Why Should We
Obey the Law?

Political Theory Today

George Klosko

Why Should We Obey the Law?

polity

First published in 2019 by Polity Press

Polity Press
65 Bridge Street
Cambridge CB2 1UR, UK

Polity Press
101 Station Landing
Suite 300
Medford, MA 02155, USA

ISBN-13: 978-1-5095-2120-3
ISBN-13: 978-1-5095-2121-0 (pb)

A catalogue record for this book is available from the British Library.

Library of Congress Cataloging-in-Publication Data

Names: Klosko, George, author.
Title: Why should we obey the law? / George Klosko.
Description: Cambridge, UK ; Medford, MA, USA : Polity Press, 2018. | Series:
    Political theory today | Includes bibliographical references and index.
Identifiers: LCCN 2018019543 (print) | LCCN 2018034583 (ebook) | ISBN
    9781509521241 (Epub) | ISBN 9781509521203 (hardback) | ISBN
9781509521210
    (pb)
Subjects: LCSH: Obedience (Law) | Political obligation. | Law--Philosophy.
Classification: LCC K250 (ebook) | LCC K250 .K56 2018 (print) | DDC
    323.6/5--dc23
LC record available at https://lccn.loc.gov/2018019543

Typeset in 11 on 15 Sabon by Servis Filmsetting Ltd, Stockport, Cheshire
Printed and bound in the United Kingdom by Clays Ltd, Elcograph S.p.A.

For further information on Polity, visit our website: politybooks.com

Contents

Acknowledgments

I have been working on questions of political obligation since the mid-1980s. I am grateful to the many colleagues and friends with whom I have discussed the subject and the many audiences to whom I have presented material. I am also indebted to the students in classes on political obligation that I have taught. Although I will not attempt to recount all the personal debts I have accumulated over the years, I should note John Simmons, whose work prompted my first interest in the subject, and, along with that of other scholars – many of whom are listed in the references – has been a continuing source of inspiration. At Polity I am grateful to the anonymous readers of my initial prospectus, and of the complete manuscript. My editor, George Owers, has been immensely helpful throughout, and I would like to thank Justin Dyer for excellent copy-editing.

Acknowledgments

Much of the material in this work is based on my previous publications, some of which are listed in the references. Given length limitations for books in this series, I am unable to present detailed arguments for many positions I defend. These are in the main found in my previous work. In a few places, I draw directly on previous publications. Material from Chapter 2 can be found in "Consent Theory of Political Obligation," in *Routledge Handbook on the Ethics of Consent*, Andreas Müller and Peter Schaber, eds. (Abingdon: Routledge, 2018). Chapter 3 draws on *The Principle of Fairness and Political Obligation* (Savage, Md.: Rowman & Littlefield Publishers, 1992) and my earliest articles. Chapter 4 draws on "Multiple Principles of Political Obligation," *Political Theory*, 32 (2004), 801–24. I am grateful to the publishers for permission to use material from these pieces here.

As ever I am grateful to my wife, Meg, my daughters, Caroline, Susanna, and Deborah, and my grandson, Manny, for moral support.

For my fellow scholars who work
on political obligation.

1

Introduction

You are walking down the street. A gunman points a pistol at you, and demands that you turn over your wallet. Chances are you will comply. In such a case, it is clear that you are *obliged* to surrender your wallet. By this, we mean that the consequences of not doing so are sufficiently unpleasant to elicit your cooperation. Consider an alternative case. Your government institutes an income tax and demands that you pay it. In this case too, chances are that you will comply. Your government has the means to force you to pay and to punish you if you do not. In this case too, you are obliged to cooperate. But this case differs in a fundamental way. If you are a citizen of the relevant state – or perhaps an inhabitant of the relevant country – it may well be that you *should* comply, that, unlike with the gunman, it is *right* that you do so. Put a bit differently, in this case, your government has a moral claim that you obey its commands. If this is true, then you are not only obliged to obey but also have an *obligation* to. If paying taxes is the law of the land, then you should obey the law and pay your taxes (see Hart 1961, 80–8).

The subject of this book, as indicated in its title, is reasons why people should obey their governments, or obey the law. The two examples in the previous paragraph differ in regard to the non-existence or existence of a moral basis for obedience. Our main questions concern the nature of this moral claim.

Political obligation, as the subject is generally referred to, is a practical topic that affects all of us and throughout our lives. Governments are constantly making laws and demanding that people obey. Confronted with a particular tax, the self-conscious citizen should ask herself whether she should pay it. The law's requirement that she do so is a factor in her practical reasoning, to be weighed against and considered along with others. The law's demands may be relatively trivial: to cross the street only at the crosswalk, or to wait for the walk sign before crossing. But far more onerous demands are possible: to pay income taxes that can amount to a substantial portion of one's earnings; in the extreme case, to provide military service that could cost one's life. In these and other instances, governments have means to enforce compliance. Ordinarily, the citizen will be obliged to comply. But once again, we should inquire into reasons that could make it *right* for her to do so. This large question encompasses numerous sub-questions: why a government has a right to its subjects' obedience; over whom such a right holds; when it holds and when it ceases to hold; the circumstances responsible for the latter; one's recourse if one is no longer obligated to obey; and many others. These questions have been central to political philosophy since the origin of the discipline. Greater and lesser thinkers have discussed them endlessly, from different perspectives, coming to sharply different conclusions. At the present time, scholars disagree, and consensus is not in sight. But, once again, these are questions with which all of us must deal, and I will attempt to provide answers. Given disagreements between scholars, I do not expect these answers to meet with general – or perhaps even widespread – acceptance. But I will attempt to present a plausible position – although one that also differs in important ways from many others in the literature.

In ordinary discourse, an "obligation" is a moral requirement that someone imposes on herself. If I promise you to take you to the movies, this requirement, created by the promise, is binding on me because I made it. Presumably, had I not made the promise, I would not have an obligation to take you. However, the term "obligation" may be used in a broader sense, in which it is roughly equivalent to "duty," with both terms referring to moral requirements that may or may not be self-imposed. Accordingly, the term "political obligation" is also used in a somewhat broad sense, denoting moral requirements to obey the law, whether or not they are self-imposed. Moral requirements to obey the law can have different bases. What I view as the most important will be discussed below.

Although scholars disagree about a great deal in regard to political obligations, they are generally in agreement on certain features a successful theory of political obligation should possess.[1] It should be "general," or account for the obligations of all or most inhabitants of the given country. Because political obligations are ordinarily owed to one's own country, an adequate theory should account for this dimension of "particularity." In addition, political obligations should be "comprehensive." They should explain moral requirements to obey

---

[1] For these conditions, see Simmons, 1979, chap. 1; Klosko 2005, 9–12.

all laws – or all legitimate laws – of the country in question.

Because in the liberal tradition, political obligations are generally viewed as of limited force, a successful theory should account for this. Although a political obligation should be viewed as a strong reason to do what the obligation requires, this reason is not necessarily conclusive or decisive. This feature of political obligations is indicated by calling them *prima facie* or *pro tanto,* with these terms indicating that the obligations in question can be overridden by countervailing considerations. This is a feature of obligations in general, besides political obligations. For instance, assume that Anne promises to meet Ben after class. On the way to the meeting, she sees Charles, who is having a heart attack. By rushing Charles to the hospital, she could save his life. Clearly, under these circumstances, her obligation to Ben is outweighed by stronger moral considerations, and so Anne would be wrong to keep the appointment. But although the moral requirement generated by the promise is outweighed by a duty to save a life, this does not imply that the former was not a genuine obligation. Evidence that it was a genuine obligation is the fact that Anne would owe Ben an apology for missing their meeting. But evidence that she had done the right thing is that Ben would be wrong not to accept her apology. Similarly, in regard to political obligations, while they ordinarily constitute strong reasons to obey the law, they too can be overridden by other factors, in which case it could actually be wrong to obey.

An additional important feature of political obligations is "content-independence." This amounts to obeying the law *because it is the law*, instead of, or along with, other reasons. In reasonably just states, the law generally overlaps with morality. What it is moral to do is supported by law; what is immoral is opposed. Thus there are generally good reasons to behave in accordance with law. For instance, there are good reasons not to assault other people, while the law makes assault illegal and subject to penalties. And so, if you refrain from assault, are you *obeying* the law or merely *complying* with it? In other words, are you obeying the law because it is the law or for other reasons? Scholars generally hold that a successful theory of obligation should explain why the law itself claims our obedience. An implication of content-independence is that there may be no direct relationship between the content of given obligations and the moral reasons why they bind (Hart 1958, 1982). In this respect, political obligations resemble promises. If

I promise to give you $10, the requirement to pay this amount is created by the promise and would not exist otherwise. If I had promised to give you $5, or $50, I would owe these amounts. Similarly, if the government institutes a sales tax rather than an income tax, your obligation will be to pay that. If it decides on a consumption tax, then your obligation will lie in that direction. In these cases, the subject's obligations do not depend on the relative merits of different forms of taxes but on the laws that have been enacted.

Construing political obligations as content-independent has a long provenance, dating back at least to the time of Thomas Hobbes (mid-seventeenth century). According to Hobbes: "Command is where a man saith, *Doe this* or *Doe not this*, without expecting other reason than the Will of him that sayes it" (1991 [1651], 176). Important aspects of political obligations follow from this view. Since moral requirements to obey laws depend on the means through which they are made rather than their content, legislators have great discretion in regard to areas in which they can legislate, and are able to establish obligations to obey all the laws they make. This reasoning is bound up with the comprehensiveness requirement noted above.

If we take a step back and consider all these requirements, we will see that they comprise a demanding list. A successful theory should explain the moral requirements of all or virtually all inhabitants of a given country to obey all the legitimate laws of their country. These requirements should be of limited force and should be content-independent: there should be reasons why subjects should obey the law because it is the law. At the present time, difficulties satisfying these requirements have called into question the existence of a suitable theory of obligation. As we will see in subsequent chapters, I believe these difficulties raise questions about the requirements themselves, whether a successful theory should be required to satisfy all of them.

Theories of political obligation are closely bound up with basic beliefs about society and government. People in Western societies generally believe that governments are necessary, that they perform services citizens need. These include providing law and order, defense from outside aggression, and the innumerable things that modern governments do in order to improve the lives of their citizens: for example, providing social welfare programs, health insurance, public parks, universities, and museums. In the history of political theory, the most celebrated account of life without government is that of Hobbes, most famously expressed in *Leviathan*. Without government, according to Hobbes, human beings experience a "war of all against all," in which the life of man is "solitary, poor, nasty, brutish, and short" (Hobbes 1991 [1651], 89). While I believe that assumptions concerning the need for government are widely if not universally held in modern Western societies, there are dissenters, mainly anarchists of some stripe or other. Their view has significant consequences for political obligations. According to anarchists, we could get along tolerably well without government, better in fact than we do with it. They therefore argue against moral requirements to obey government – with some going further and contending that we are required to fight against it. If government is in fact not necessary, it seems unlikely if not impossible that we can develop convincing arguments why people should obey it.

Throughout this volume, I reject the claims of anarchists and assume that the state is necessary (see Klosko 2005, chap. 2). To defend this position, one need not go to the extremes of Hobbes. As James Madison says in the *Federalist Papers* (#51), if men were angels, government would not be necessary. But men are not angels, and so must be constrained. This is so, even if we assume that people are basically reasonable and not the ruthless creatures of Hobbes's imagination. Even if people are basically well meaning, it is frequently in their interest to pursue their own good at the expense of other people. Familiar examples concern public goods, which people will receive whether or not they pay for them. And so they have incentives not to: for example, not to pay their taxes, if they can get away with this. Even if incentives align, in a diverse society, people will disagree about the best way to pursue cooperative projects, which makes government necessary to arrive at solutions – and democratic practices for decisions to be made fairly. In addition, psychological research has established that people are liable to cognitive errors. These are discussed briefly, in Chapter 4. For instance, "self-enhancement bias" leads people to overestimate their own capabilities and to underestimate their own incompetence and other limitations. This and additional similar tendencies have been thoroughly documented empirically. Accordingly, even if people are well meaning, their judgment is often flawed, and it is necessary to subject their reasoning to the law.

A second, related, issue is more controversial: how well government can function if people do not have political obligations. I believe that most people believe that, like government itself, political obligations are necessary and that they have obligations (esp. Tyler 1990; Klosko 2005, chaps. 9–10; cf. Green 1996). Evidence of people's beliefs on this question is scant, but common practices support the view that most people believe that governments require willing cooperation from those they govern, that governments ruling through force alone could not provide the services that people require. For example, consider payment of income tax in the United States. Compliance is largely voluntary. Studies show that more than 80% of people comply voluntarily (IRS Oversight Board n.d.). It seems unlikely that so many people would behave in this way unless they thought it was their duty to do so. Tax payments are of course not entirely voluntary. The Internal Revenue Service oversees the tax system and enforces compliance. But because of its limited resources, the IRS audits only a small percentage of returns. If fear of being punished for non-payment was people's sole reason for compliance, we may presume that far fewer people would pay their taxes. Many functions of government involve coordinating the behavior of large numbers of people. Could these functions be performed adequately if people believed they did not have moral requirements to cooperate with government's commands, including accepting government's decisions concerning the form these functions should take? But once again, there are dissenters. In the recent literature, important theorists argue that obligations are not necessary. Although they believe in the need for government, they hold that government would be able to fulfill its functions without people believing they were morally required to go along with it (e.g., Simmons 1979, chap. 8; cf. Huemer 2012).

On the whole, the empirical assumptions I make in this study are familiar and, I believe, commonsensical. They should be accepted by most readers, although theorists and scholars disagree with some or all of them. Once again, to a good degree, disagreements about political obligations can be traced back to them. Thus it is important to bear in mind basic premises on which the argument in this volume rests and how they work themselves out in the arguments we develop.

2

Consent Theory

In the Western tradition, perhaps the most familiar answer to questions of political obligation is a theory based on consent. This is a common feature of popular discourse and important public documents. For instance, according to the Declaration of Independence, governments derive "their just powers from the consent of the governed." In this chapter, we will examine this view in some detail, not only in order to understand consent itself, but also as an example of the considerations that support and undermine different theories of obligation.

Consent

The doctrine of consent first arose in late medieval times in connection with royal authorities' need to secure the agreement of other grandees to their plans or projects (Klosko 2011b). In a simple case, a king would summon nobles who would be asked to agree to a plan to raise taxes or undertake some war. Although the king would ordinarily have to make concessions in order to secure the nobles' consent, the fact that they had consented would strengthen his position. Similarly, according to a consent theory of political obligation, when people surrender their power to government, this is done on certain conditions. They enter into a contractual relationship with government – "the social contract" – agreeing to obey it as long as it performs the specific functions for which it was established.

Central to the idea of consent is change to the normative status of the persons to whom consent is given, generally by according them rights they did not previously have. Ordinarily, your taking my car without permission would not be justified, would possibly even be a crime. But circumstances would be different if I consented to let you use it. My consent would give you a right to use the car. As a general rule, consent must be given freely – on which more directly – and communicated to the relevant parties. Ordinarily, you would not acquire a right to use my car unless I somehow let you know that you had the right. In this respect, an act of consent is like a promise, as, ordinarily, promises too must be communicated to the parties to whom they are given.

Like promises and other "obligations" in the narrow or technical sense, moral requirements based on consent are imposed by individuals upon themselves. This is one of consent theory's chief attractions. The idea that people must agree to their obligations to government is supported by the great weight liberal political theory places on values of liberty and autonomy. As Harry Beran puts this, rights to self-determination should extend to political self-determination. People should be under political authority only if they put themselves under it (Beran 1987). Presumably because of its intuitive clarity, consenting to obey government is highly attractive as a means through which political obligations are assumed. According to John Locke, it is a basis that "[n]obody doubts" (1988 [1690], sec. 119). In his essay "Of the Original Contract," David Hume supports this view: where consent "has place," he writes, "[i]t is surely the best and most sacred of any." But Hume also notes that "it has very seldom had place in any degree" (1985 [1748], 474). As we will see, establishing that consent actually "has place" is the doctrine's chief weakness.

Like promises, consent to government is thought to bind only if certain conditions are met. We will focus on three conditions which are especially prominent. First, the promisor must not be forced to make the promise. She must do so freely, and so must have reasonable alternatives to making it. Second, she must be aware of what the promise entails. This includes such matters as exactly how the promise is made, to whom it is made, and to what it commits the promisor. Third, the promisor must be competent to make it. Generally, this includes age requirements, while similar restrictions hold in regard to various psychological conditions, including mental illness and intoxication. If any of these conditions is not satisfied, a given promise will not create a binding obligation. Accordingly, these conditions may be described as "defeating conditions," as failure to satisfy one or more of them will generally prevent a binding promise from being completed (Beran 1987, 5–9). Although various additional conditions could be noted, in general, if Abe makes some promise to Beth, we may presume that the promise is valid, unless it can be shown that one or more of the defeating conditions is present. As we will see, analogous defeating conditions play a significant role in the consent theory of political obligation.

The *locus classicus* for a consent theory of political obligation is John Locke's *Second Treatise of Government*, which is one of the most familiar accounts of political obligation in the liberal tradition. A brief look at Locke's doctrine provides an overview of both strengths and weaknesses of consent theory and reasons for its continuing relevance. According to Locke, people are by nature free. They originally exist in a state of nature, which is a situation without government. Because people are naturally free, nothing can remove them from this condition but their own consent (Locke 1988 [1690], sec. 95). People in this condition are subject to the law of nature. But because there is no authority to enforce this law, Locke subscribes to the "strange Doctrine" (sec. 13) that all men have the right to enforce it for themselves. While the state of nature is relatively peaceful, self-enforcement leads to conflict, and so people are willing to surrender this power and establish government, which they do by consenting to join together in political society and agreeing "to be concluded by the majority" (sec. 96).

The advantages of Locke's theory are apparent. In addition to its intuitive clarity, consent provides a clear basis for content-independence. In leaving the state of nature and consenting to be concluded

by the majority, a given individual, Abe, undertakes an obligation to do whatever the majority
decides – though not without limits, on which more
directly. As noted above, this feature grounds political obligations that are comprehensive. Moreover,
consent theory has the great advantage of accounting for what Leslie Green calls "the self-image of
the state." As Green says, the state conceives of
itself as a "duty imposer." By issuing directives, it is
able to change people's normative status, to impose
duties and other requirements on them, the content
of which it alone determines (Green 1988, 86). The
state's ability to do this follows from people's agreement to be concluded by what the majority decides.
As Green also argues, other theories of political
obligation encounter difficulties accounting for this
feature of political obligations, which is presumably
a strong reason for the continuing attraction of
consent theory.

An additional strength of consent theory is its
ability to explain exactly how the powers of government are limited. The scope of government's
legitimate power is built into the terms according to
which people consent. If government violates these
terms or oversteps in other ways, it loses its powers
and its subjects have various recourse. One reason
for the continuing appeal of consent theory is its

ability to justify taking action against governments that are viewed as unjust, as in Locke's *Second Treatise* and the Declaration of Independence.

At first sight, Locke's doctrine of consent provides strong protection for individual liberty. Political obligations require personal consent. One is not bound by the consent of one's father, or by the terms of an original contract made at the foundation of society. Each individual must agree himself (Locke 1988 [1690], secs. 116–18). However, although "express consent" establishes clear political bonds, Locke recognizes that few people consent in this way. And so he turns to what he calls "tacit consent," other actions that people perform that are capable of binding them.

The need for tacit consent is clear. In general, in modern societies, the only people who may be viewed as consenting expressly are naturalized citizens, who voluntarily move from country A to country B. If they become citizens of B, this ordinarily entails taking an explicit oath of obedience to their new government. In addition, in most cases, they can be taken to have moved voluntarily and voluntarily chosen to become citizens of B, thereby freely assuming obligations to B. But because naturalized citizens generally constitute only a small fraction of society, most inhabitants must be covered by tacit consent. For all intents and purpose, the consent theory of political obligation is a theory of tacit consent. As Locke views it, tacit consent is expansive:

> And to this I say that every Man, that hath any Possession, or Enjoyment of any part of the Dominions of any Government, doth thereby give his tacit Consent, and is as far forth obliged to Obedience to the Laws of that Government, during such Enjoyment, as any one under it; whether this his Possession be of Land, to him and his Heirs for ever, or a Lodging only for a Week; or whether it be barely traveling freely on the Highway; and in Effect, it reaches as far as the very being of any one within the Territories of that Government. (1988 [1690], sec. 119)

The actions Locke lists would account for the political obligations of all or virtually all inhabitants of the relevant territory. However, his view confronts severe difficulties. Careful examination of exactly what constitutes tacit consent reveals that, like express consent, it has difficulties accounting for the obligations of more than a fraction of society.

In a celebrated study of tacit consent, A. John Simmons argues that, in its essential characteristics, it is equivalent to express consent (1979, chap.

4). Although the means through which it is communicated differ from those in express consent, because it is still consent, it must possess the main characteristics of any act of consent. Distinctive of tacit consent is that it is communicated through inaction rather than by action. For instance, imagine that I tell my class that I am going to reschedule an examination unless anyone objects, and I give them adequate opportunity to speak up. If no one raises an objection, then I may take it that they have agreed, although no one has explicitly said so. Consideration of such examples indicates the role of defeating conditions. In this case, competence may be assumed. More important, for the students' tacit consent to be binding they must not be forced to give it. They must consent voluntarily. In addition, as Simmons says, the means of expressing lack of consent should not be unduly difficult to perform (1979, 81). Thus if I tell my students that, rather than expressing themselves verbally, the means through which they should object is by doing standing backflips, their failure to perform this action would ordinarily not be viewed as constituting consent. For tacit consent, the awareness requirements are especially significant. One must not only not be forced to consent, but one must also be aware that tacit consent is called for and how one goes about giving it or not giving it. One must be aware of the period of time – if there is one – during which one may or may not consent. One must also be aware of what one would be committing oneself to, as would be true of a promise, and the fact that this commitment would not exist unless one consented. In the example of rescheduling my examination, these conditions may be presumed to be satisfied, and the students' tacit consent is not problematic. But circumstances in regard to political obligations are more complex. Defeating conditions cause severe difficulties for acts that have been claimed to constitute tacit consent.

Consider staying in one's country, which is widely viewed as the most plausible basis – as in Locke's theory. Most people are probably aware that if they remain in a given country, they will be required to obey its laws, while this requirement will no longer obtain if they leave. Along similar lines, most people probably recognize that they undertake similar requirements when they voluntarily enter another country. For instance, a tourist entering Canada is probably aware that, if she drives, she must abide by Canadian traffic laws and may be required to pay fines if she does not. But do these considerations support the view that staying in one's country and not emigrating to another constitutes consent to obey its laws? In order for this conclusion to hold, failure to leave must not fall foul of the defeating conditions. However, how many people actually believe that continued residence constitutes consent? Unlike naturalized citizens, most people are simply born into their societies and live there largely because they have always lived there. They probably recognize that, if they leave country A for country B, they will no longer have requirements to obey the laws of A. But it seems unlikely that they recognize that tacit consent is called for or that there is a definite period of time in which to consent or not to. Severe problems follow from the voluntariness requirement. Hanging over this form of tacit consent is the criticism of Hume, who rejects the doctrine, because the means of expressing lack of consent are not ordinarily available:

> Can we seriously say that a poor peasant or artizan has a free choice to leave his country, when he knows no foreign language or manners, and lives from day to day, by the small wages which he acquires? We may as well assert, that a man, by remaining in a vessel, freely consents to the dominion of the master, though he was carried on board while asleep, and must leap into the ocean, and perish, the moment he leaves her. (1985 [1748], 475)

Certainly, continued residence does not constitute tacit consent if one is actively prevented from leaving, for example if borders are closed and guarded, as in the former East Germany. But as Hume says, even if borders are open, for many people it may not be possible to leave, while others would find the costs of leaving prohibitively high. If Abe is to leave country A, another country must be willing to take him. Even then, financial costs of moving could be prohibitively high, while he must be able to function adequately in B. For instance, he must know the language, be able to find a job, and so on. Even if all these conditions are satisfied, it still may be extremely difficult to leave. As Simmons argues, much of what is precious in life cannot be taken with one: family, friends, a particular culture (1979, 99). Therefore, choice of either leaving or consenting tacitly could well be viewed as coercive.

Given the problems with continued residence, theorists have identified other actions that might serve. An attractive possibility is voting. If Beth votes in an election, one could argue that she has agreed to be governed by the winners, and so to obey the law (Plamenatz 1968, 168–71; Singer 1973). This argument is supported by an analogy with games. If Beth starts to play chess with another person, she is ordinarily viewed as agreeing to abide by its rules. But this analogy takes us only so far. First of all, in the United States, many citizens do not vote. The vote in the 2016 presidential election was around 60%, which is actually high for US elections (United States Elections Project n.d.). But does this mean that the 40% of citizens who did not vote do not have political obligations? In order to make the argument bind most or all citizens, we must move from the act of voting to possessing the right to vote as constituting tacit consent. But on this line of reasoning, the voluntary action that is central to consent is left behind. In regard to voting, knowledge requirements are especially damaging. It is unlikely that many people vote with the idea that, by doing so, they are agreeing to obey the laws of their countries, and that, if they did not vote, they would not have obligations to do so. How many people would vote if they realized that, by not voting, they would free themselves from moral requirements to obey the law, including, for example, requirements to pay their taxes? It seems clear that these and perhaps other knowledge conditions prevent voting from constituting tacit consent to obey the law. Although it may seem that someone who votes is, among other things, expressing support for her political system, this is not enough for voting to ground political obligations.

To use a distinction of Simmons', we may say that voting is "consent implying" (1979, 88–91). By this, Simmons means that voting is the kind of act one would ordinarily perform only if one had consented to obey the law. But in spite of this, it itself does not constitute consent.

Other actions that are widely performed have been advanced by theorists as constituting consent to government. Examples include saying the Pledge of Allegiance or taking the appropriate oath upon joining the armed forces. But if we carefully assess these actions against the necessary conditions, we will likely conclude that they too come up short. In particular, it is highly unlikely that many people perform these acts with the intention of binding themselves to obey the law, with the understanding that, if they did not do so, they would not have moral requirements to obey.[1]

In view of these and other difficulties, the idea that political obligations rest on consent has been largely rejected by contemporary scholars. Although, as Locke and Hume note, the idea is highly attractive when the conditions for consent are met, they are not met for almost all citizens of contemporary

---

[1] For discussion of other possibilities, including "reformist" consent, see Klosko 1991.

countries. Thus consent is thought to fail the test of "generality," accounting for the obligations of all or most all citizens.

Hypothetical Consent

In response to the difficulties of tacit consent, theorists have extended what they mean by consent. One possibility is that the consent in question need not actually be performed. Instead, if conditions in one's country are such that one *would* consent to obey the laws if given the opportunity to do so, then this hypothetical consent could ground moral requirements to obey the law. Historically, a position along these lines can be traced back to Immanuel Kant, who contends that government's power is limited by the requirement that the legislator should "frame his laws in such a way that they could have been produced by the united will of a whole nation" (1970 [1793], 79). In a celebrated article, Jeremy Waldron argues that a conception of hypothetical consent underlies fundamental commitments of liberal political theory. Waldron views the liberal mindset as rejecting "tradition, mystery, awe and superstition as the basis of order" (1987, 134). Because of its determination to subject authority to requirements of reason, liberalism requires that laws be *transparent*. Society's fundamental principles should be capable of being understood by all individuals who are subject to them (Waldron 1987, 146). However, as bases for political obligation, these conceptions of hypothetical consent are subject to criticism. To use the words of Ronald Dworkin: "A hypothetical contract is not simply a pale form of an actual contract; it is no contract at all" (1977, 151). For example, the fact that Abe would agree to marry some famous Hollywood actress if given the chance does not mean that he has obligations to her as if he had actually married her. There are cases in which hypothetical consent may operate. For instance, if you come across someone who has passed out and fallen into a pond, ordinarily you may presume that the person would consent to have you rescue him, if he were able to do so. In a case along these lines, hypothetical consent is necessary, because the person is unconscious and unable actually to consent. But in regard to political obligations, we may assume that the vast majority of people are not prevented from providing actual consent by physical or mental incapacities. In their cases, the fact that the laws are such that they would consent to them under some circumstances does not entail that they actually have consented.

These considerations tell against hypothetical

consent as a basis for political obligations. Rather than grounding obligations to obey the law, it is a useful device for assessing the moral quality of the laws, whether they should be viewed as legitimate or the kind of laws it would be acceptable to obey, but again, not as the actual basis for requirements to obey. Hypothetical consent performs a useful service in drawing attention away from voluntary actions performed or supposedly performed by citizens in order to assume political obligations to aspects of the political system that would justify consenting to it. But because it itself is not able to establish moral requirements to obey the law, if it is to ground these, it must be supplemented by additional moral principles.

Assessment

In spite of the difficulties we have seen, consent appears to retain a strong hold on public consciousness. As it seems to me, a lasting legacy of consent theory is shaping the way we view political obligations. If one returns to the conditions for a successful theory of obligation in Chapter 1, one will note that all of these are satisfied by consent – with of course the exception of generality. Its central role in determining how we think of political obligations is likely one reason for its continuing hold. As we have noted, obligations based on consent not only follow from a clear moral principle, but are also comprehensive, limited in force, and owed to a particular political society – the one to which one consents. Especially important is the open-ended character of consent. As noted above, according to Locke, consent to government binds one "to be concluded by the majority." Whatever the majority decides is therefore binding. This feature of consent supports both the content-independence of political obligations and the "self-image of the state," that the state is a "duty imposer," with all inhabitants bound by whatever it decides. As it seems to me, consent has played an important role in supporting the idea that a successful theory of political obligation should satisfy these conditions. Given its place as the first significant theory of political obligation in the West, it is likely that obligations based on consent came to be viewed as a kind of model for obligations in general. These features of consent became lodged in theorists' minds as conditions that all legitimate theories of obligation should meet.[2]

---

[2] As an anonymous reviewer suggests, consent may also be responsible for the popular belief that political obligations require voluntary commitment.

This last point raises what I view as a serious difficulty resulting from the legacy of consent. I believe it sets the bar too high. In recent decades, repeated unsuccessful efforts by theorists have shown that this set of demands is extremely difficult to meet, so much so that it is likely that no traditional theory of obligation is able to do so. As theorists have confronted this realization, they have come to question the possibility of a successful theory of obligation at all. The view that there is no successful theory is probably now the dominant position in the literature (see Simmons 1979; Smith 1973; Raz 1989). But this view of course depends heavily on what we mean by success. Questioning and revising the traditional criteria could well allow us to craft a theory that we should regard as successful, even though it does not measure up to traditional requirements. Accordingly, as we will see in subsequent chapters, breaking consent's continuing hold may be necessary if we are to focus on a theory of political obligation that is able to succeed at the doctrine's practical task. This is providing moral reasons why people should obey the laws of their countries, without requiring that it satisfy additional requirements of content-independence and support the "self-image of the state." In other words, with this legacy of consent cast aside, I believe a theory can be worked out that we should accept as satisfactory.

3

The Principle of Fair Play

The problems we have seen with consent theory indicate the difficulty of grounding obligations to obey the law on citizens' voluntary acts. Whatever acts we identify, as with both express and tacit consent, it is unlikely that most citizens have performed them. But moral requirements voluntarily assumed do not exhaust the possibilities, and it is in this direction that we turn.

Consequentialism

In a consequentialist moral theory, the moral worth of an action is assessed in terms of its consequences (however we measure these, i.e., in regard to pleasure, satisfied desire, or some other metric). The right action is one with foreseeable consequences at least as good as those of any other possible action.

Consequentialism provides a commonsense alternative to consent. The central idea is that we should obey the law because of the beneficial consequences of doing so and adverse consequences of disobedience. In the first in-depth discussion of political obligation in our tradition, in Plato's dialogue *Crito*, the personified Laws of Athens argue along these lines. They complain that by breaking the law and escaping from prison, Socrates would destroy the state (*Crito* 50a–b). As we will see, the particular factual claim underlying this argument is difficult to sustain, but if it is true that disobedience would in fact damage the state, then we would have strong reasons why people should obey the law, and the problem of political obligation would be largely solved.

One reason why this position may seem plausible is that disobedience of many laws has obvious detrimental consequences. As noted above, the law generally overlaps with morality. It is against the law to assault other people. If Abe assaults Beth, he obviously causes harm and so does something wrong. But other laws are not of this type. In many cases, the law contributes to the good of society by coordinating the actions of large numbers of people. Familiar examples are traffic laws. It is necessary that all drivers obey a uniform set of rules. These are codified in law, with violations enforced. In innumerable ways, coordination enforced by law contributes to the smooth functioning of society, including allowing essential needs to be met. However, in many cases, individual obedience of coordination laws tells against consequentialism. In a large society, there are circumstances in which one person's cooperation or non-cooperation will not affect the workings of society and not affect the benefits or burdens of other people. Imagine a cooperative enterprise that is not large. My two neighbors and I share a well, which is running out of water. We mandate that, until this difficult time passes, we are not allowed to water our lawns. Disregarding this decision, I wait until it gets dark and water my lawn every night. This would presumably cause us to run out of water sooner and so directly harm my neighbors. But change the scale of the example. Imagine that our entire city of 1,000,000 people is running short of water, and officials pass a similar ban on lawn watering. Assume that coordinating everyone's actions in this way will effectively manage the crisis. Once again I do not cooperate. But in this case, because of the scale of the enterprise, the amount of extra water I use will not be noticeable and so will not affect any other residents.

To make matters worse for consequentialism, in many cases such as these, the consequences of disobedience by a small number of people are actually *better* than those of universal compliance. Once again, imagine a large city that has imposed severe water restrictions. If I break the law by watering my lawn or take showers that are longer than mandated, there is an immediate sense in which I benefit. Although I use more water than is allowed, it is not clear why this is wrong, since my overuse is not noticeable and so does not hurt anyone else. In a case such as this, the paradoxical conclusion follows that it is not only in my interest that I break the law, but also in the interest of society. On consequentialist premises, the interest of society is a sum of the utility levels of all its members. In this case, my breaking the rules raises my utility level without lowering that of anyone else. So not only do I gain, but so does society. Consider another example. Anne does not pay her income taxes, thereby violating the tax laws. Once again, her conduct benefits herself. If she does not pay, she will have an extra ten or twenty thousand dollars with which to buy lavish presents for her friends or family. Given the size of the US federal budget – some four trillion dollars, with a deficit in the hundreds of billions – her non-contribution will not be noticeable and so will not hurt anyone else. By violating the tax laws, Anne too raises the utility level of society. Or imagine that Beth is contributing to air pollution by not fixing the catalytic converter on her car. Once again, in a large society, her transgression will not be noticeable. The most sensitive scientific instruments would be unable to detect the difference in air quality caused by her conduct. And so once again, why it is wrong for Beth not to comply? If fixing catalytic converters is expensive and not fixing hers leaves her with additional money that she can use to bring pleasure to herself and to other people, why should she fix it? There is of course a possible rub. In cases such as these, if large numbers of other people also break the law, the results could be catastrophic. If large numbers of Americans stop paying their taxes, the government will lack adequate funds, and the results could be dire indeed. Similarly, if large number of inhabitants violate air pollution laws or water restrictions, the community as a whole could suffer severely.

As these examples show, consequentialism is beset by paradoxical cases in which certain conduct by large numbers of people would be damaging to society, although if performed by only a small number, the consequences would actually be beneficial (Harrod 1936). Accordingly, a familiar way to argue that I would do wrong in overusing water or not paying my taxes is to appeal to the consequences if *everyone* behaved similarly. Upon discovering that Anne has not paid her taxes, a commonsense retort is: "What if everyone did that?" Once again, if everyone did in fact behave similarly, the consequences could be severe. But there is a problem with this response: it is highly unlikely that everyone will in fact behave similarly (see Broad 1915–16), while there is ordinarily no reason to believe that Anne's non-compliance will cause large numbers of others to behave similarly.

Consequentialism's problems with these cases are compounded by our intuitive response to them. In the three cases I have noted, it is intuitively clear that the subjects are behaving wrongly. They are not only disobeying the law, but we also strongly feel that they are cheating. What they are doing is unfair or unjust. Given that consequentialism cannot account for this, the nature of their wrong-doing must be sought elsewhere.

Fair Play

I assume that the reader will agree that Anne is doing something wrong in not paying her taxes, and the same is true in the other examples, even though consequentialism cannot explain this. This problem indicates the advantages of the principle of fair play (or the principle of fairness). Return to Beth and her catalytic converter. As we have seen, because general but not universal adherence to anti-pollution laws is necessary, it is actually better for society, as of course for Beth herself, if she disobeys them. But one could ask why Beth rather than other citizens should receive the benefit of non-compliance. Assume that air quality will be acceptable if 95% of people use catalytic converters. On consequentialist reasoning, then, it is wrong if everyone complies, as that would require that 5% of the population bear costly burdens that are unnecessary. To maximize utility, 95% of people should comply and 5% enjoy the advantages of not doing so. But which 5%? Why should some people benefit from clean air provided by the sacrifices of their fellow citizens without making similar sacrifices themselves? If adherence to the rules of some public policy benefits everyone, then everyone should obey them. Our moral intuitions include concerns of fairness as well as utility (Lyons 1965, chap. 5).

In cases of this sort, the benefits of non-compliance can be distributed fairly. We could employ some fair procedure or mechanism to decide who does not have to comply. A familiar example is a draft lottery. If the nation's armed forces require that 25% of young men and women serve and we assume that service is costly, it would detract from the welfare of society if everyone served. A mechanism could therefore be implemented to choose which 25% must serve, through a draft lottery or some other fair procedure. This seems clearly preferable to allowing some people to avoid service while others serve, simply because the former are not patriotic. Since a draft lottery is a fair way to distribute the burdens of military service and the benefits of not having to serve, it would be unfair for Abe not to serve without taking part in the lottery. As long as he has no convincing reason why he rather than other people should not have to serve, if he unilaterally seizes the benefits of non-service, he will be taking advantage of his fellow citizens and so wronging them. In other words, he will be free-riding. Along similar lines, in the examples above, it is not fair for Anne and Beth simply to allocate additional benefits to themselves. Since most or all citizens would presumably prefer not to comply with the measures noted, because of their unilateral non-compliance, Anne and Beth are also free-riding. Hence the principle of fair play. In cases in which a given population enjoys benefits produced by costly sacrifices of its members, it is unfair for a given individual who enjoys the benefits simply to assume for herself the additional benefits of non-compliance. Because it would be wrong for me simply to take more than the allotted amount of water or for Beth simply not to use a catalytic converter or for Anne not to pay her taxes, all three of us should obey the law and bear the burdens in question.

The principle of fair play is a more promising basis for political obligations than the other two principles we have looked at. I believe it is able to ground a core of political obligations for all or nearly all inhabitants of modern countries – although, as we will see, it too confronts problems. The principle was first clearly formulated by H. L. A. Hart in 1955:

> [W]hen a number of persons conduct any joint enterprise according to rules and thus restrict their liberty, those who have submitted to these restrictions when required have a right to a similar submission from those who have benefited by their submission. (1955, 185)

The moral basis of the principle is mutuality of restrictions. As illustrated in the above examples, under certain conditions, the sacrifices made by members of a cooperative scheme in order to produce benefits also benefit non-cooperators, who do not make similar sacrifices. According to the principle of fair play, this situation is unfair, and it is intended to justify the obligations of non-cooperators. The underlying moral principle at work in such cases is described as "the just distribution of benefits and burdens" (Lyons 1965, 164).

According to the principle of fair play, society is conceived as a cooperative enterprise, the members of which produce and receive benefits. In order to understand the principle's workings, we must examine different kinds of cooperative enterprises and how they work. To begin with, we must distinguish schemes that provide "excludable" and "non-excludable" benefits. Goods of the former kind can be provided to some members of a given community while being denied to others. Examples are entrance to a theater, water from a well, or countless other similar goods. As the designation indicates, non-excludable goods cannot be provided to some members of a given community but not others. Such goods, often called "public goods," include clean air and national defense.[1] If we clean

---

[1] According to the standard definition, public goods are "non-rival" as well as non-excludable. If a good is non-rival, one person's consumption does not affect the amount available to other people (as with, for example, clean air). Exactly where

up the air in a given city, ordinarily, it will not be possible for some inhabitants to benefit while others do not.

The principle of fair play is able clearly to establish obligations in regard to excludable goods. Assume that three neighbors dig a well, while a fourth, Alice, has refused to join in the work. Once the well has been dug, Alice goes over to it and takes water. This would be a clear case of free-riding. If we assume that continuing operation of the well requires continued maintenance, by helping herself to water, Alice would clearly incur an obligation to do her part in the maintenance. Similarly, if Ben's neighbors organize a pot luck supper to which each brings a dish, if Ben helps himself to food, he incurs an obligation to bring a dish. As a rule, if people accept benefits that are produced by the cooperative efforts of others, they incur obligations to share in those efforts.

However, as it concerns excludable goods, the principle of fair play is not a promising basis for political obligations. In such cases, whether a given

we draw the line between excludable and non-excludable goods is subject to argument, as the former category could also include roads, airports, and other public accommodations. But although it is possible to exclude people from their use, in practice it is often prohibitively expensive or inconvenient to do so.

individual incurs obligations will be her choice. Because it is generally possible for people not to share in given benefits, it is generally up to them to decide if they wish to take them at the cost of having to bear a fair share of the effort necessary to produce them. Thus if Alice declines to join the well-digging scheme, she will not have obligations to contribute. In cases concerned with excludable goods, the principle of fair play is closely related to a principle of consent. One will not have obligations to contribute to a given scheme unless one accepts benefits from it or otherwise joins it. But in regard to political obligation, focus on excludable goods is not very productive. Many of the most important benefits provided by government are public goods which cannot be voluntarily accepted in the usual sense.

If the principle of fair play is to make a notable contribution to questions of political obligation, it must be able to establish obligations to contribute to non-excludable goods. It is important to note that many public goods produced by the cooperative efforts of large numbers of people are vital to people's lives. Most notable are public goods bearing on physical security, including national defense and law and order. As noted, these benefits cannot be provided to some members of the community without all other members receiving them. Other similar benefits include protection from natural disasters, environmental problems, and deadly diseases. Providing these benefits and others like them is traditionally viewed as central to government's responsibilities. Because provision of these goods requires that people's activities be coordinated by the state through the law, theorists contend that the principle of fair play grounds moral requirements to obey the law as it bears on the relevant cooperative schemes. However, because the benefits in question are public goods, it is not possible for individuals to accept them and so join the schemes by doing so. If the principle of fair play is to account for the obligations of most or all citizens, it must be able to establish obligations to contribute to goods that are not accepted in the usual sense.[2]

Important theorists contend that the principle of fair play is not able to establish widespread obligations in regard to such goods (Dworkin 1986, 192–3; Rawls 1999, 97–8). This position is supported by a famous example of Robert Nozick's

---

[2] In an influential discussion, Simmons argues that public goods can be "accepted" in a sense if they are taken "knowingly and willingly," and recipients are aware of their source (1979, 132). For criticism of Simmons' view, see Klosko 1992, 50–2.

(1974, 93–6). Assume that Anne's neighborhood organizes a public-address system to provide music and other programs, and each neighbor takes a turn running the system for a day. If Anne has enjoyed listening to the system, must she give up a day when her turn comes? What if she prefers not to? Nozick argues that Anne does not have a requirement to participate. The principle of fairness does not eliminate "the need for other persons' *consenting* to cooperate and limit their own activities" (Nozick 1974, 95; his emphasis). Important scholars agree that, under these circumstances, Anne does not have an obligation to comply. But they draw various conclusions in regard to exactly how the example works and what it means for the principle of fair play. For instance, according to A. John Simmons, the reason Anne does not incur an obligation is that she is simply a bystander in regard to the public-address scheme. It has been built up around her, with no input from her. In order for her to have obligations to do her part in running it, she must be a *participant* in the scheme (Simmons 1979, 120–1). To be a participant, a subject must have particular attitudes in regard to benefits it provides. She must believe the benefits are worth their costs, and must receive them "willingly and knowingly." This last condition requires that she know that the benefits in question *are* products of a cooperative scheme, a condition that Simmons believes is not generally satisfied (1979, 138–42).

Other scholars believe that arguments along these lines can be countered. Richard Dagger argues that state benefits are in fact widely accepted. In many of their activities, citizens take advantage of facilities the state provides, such as roads and communications. Although these facilities cannot be avoided, they are used "voluntarily," taking "voluntarily" in a wider sense as meaning "not under constraint or duress" (Dagger 1997, 75). Regardless of whether a given citizen performs a particular action that constitutes acceptance of state benefits, the latter are central to their lives. Because there is a clear sense in which they have voluntarily accepted these benefits, it would be wrong for recipients not to do their part in providing them (Dagger 1997, 77).

I believe a strong case can be made that voluntary acceptance is not necessary. In my previous work (esp. Klosko 1992, chap. 2), I argue that Nozick's example seems plausible because of the trivial nature of the benefits in question. But if we consider cooperative schemes that provide far more important benefits, his reasoning will no longer hold. In order to generate obligations, a cooperative scheme that provides non-excludable goods must satisfy three conditions. The goods:

(i)   must be worth the recipients' effort in providing them;

(ii) must be presumptively beneficial: that is, they may be assumed to be indispensable for satisfactory lives (call goods that satisfy this condition "presumptive goods");

(iii) must have benefits and burdens that are fairly distributed.

As an example, consider the benefits of national defense. Because these benefits are non-excludable, Beth receives them whether or not she pursues them. In fact, because the benefits of defense are unavoidable as well as non-excludable, it is not clear how she could pursue them even if she wished to. However, because the benefits are indispensable to Beth's welfare, we may presume that she would pursue them (and bear the associated costs) if this were necessary for their receipt. If we imagine an artificial choice situation analogous to a state of nature or John Rawls's original position, it seems clear that under almost all circumstances Beth would choose to receive the benefits at the prescribed cost, if she had the choice. Because of the indispensability of national defense, it would not be rational for her to choose otherwise. But in the case under consideration, Beth's obligation to the providers of defense does not stem from hypothetical consent – that she *would* consent to receive the benefits under some circumstances – but from the fact that she receives them through the burdensome labors of other people.

Other public goods supplied by government that may also be viewed as necessary for acceptable lives include those noted above: law and order, protection from environmental hazards, natural disasters, and major threats to public health. In all these cases, because recipients may be presumed to need the benefits in question, they may also be presumed to have obligations to support the cooperative schemes that supply them. It is important to note, however, that these obligations are only *presumptive* and that such presumptions are rebuttable. If Beth can make a convincing argument that she does not benefit from national defense – for example, because she is a devout pacifist, so that the violence with which defense systems are bound up violates her religious beliefs – then she may be absolved of obligations to contribute to defense. But barring her ability to make such an argument, the obligation may be presumed to hold. Moreover, even if she were able to argue that she does not benefit from defense, because government provides a number of other public goods that are also ordinarily viewed as necessary for acceptable lives, it is likely that she would still have obligations to support government's provision of some or all of these other goods. It seems unlikely that she would be able to rebut presumptions in regard to the great benefit of all these goods, and so be absolved entirely of obligations to cooperate.

Taking a step back, we can see that the principle of fair play is like a consequentialist theory in establishing obligations to obey the law that do not depend upon people's voluntary actions. It is therefore able to avoid the problems of generality that plague consent theory. While Nozick wishes in effect to reduce the principle of fair play to a principle of consent, the position I have sketched avoids this problem. Similarly, while Simmons argues that demanding subjective attitudes are necessary to bind an individual to a cooperative scheme – once again, raising problems of generality – as long as we focus on schemes that provide presumptive goods, we are able to presume that people have obligations, without inquiring into their attitudes or beliefs. But the principle of fair play does not avoid questions concerning attitudes entirely. These may be invoked in response to presumptions of obligation. As we have seen, it is possible that Beth does not benefit from a given good, or does not benefit at an adequate level to make receiving it worth its costs. I have noted the possible response if she is a pacifist. Thus questions concerning attitudes and beliefs cannot be avoided entirely. Although their role is minimal, they still affect the generality of fair-play obligations. However, once again, it is unlikely that many people would be able to argue convincingly that they do not have defense obligations. Given the ordinary facts of human life, we may presume that almost everyone benefits from defense, and from the other presumptive goods noted – which is of course what justifies us in identifying them as presumptively beneficial. The assumption that these goods are necessary for an acceptable life is an important empirical premise of the argument from fair play (see above, pp. 8–10).

Because these benefits are necessary for an acceptable life (condition [ii] above), they are almost certainly worth their costs to all recipients, and so condition (i) is satisfied as well. The third condition, that benefits and burdens of the cooperative scheme must be distributed fairly, is more problematic. This requirement follows from the moral logic of the principle of fair play. If some cooperative scheme distributes its benefits and/or burdens in ways that benefit some individuals far more than others, it may be difficult to maintain that those who lose out in this arrangement have duties of fair play to cooperate that are grounded in the need to even out benefits and burdens. The fair-distribution requirement raises considerable complexities that cannot be explored in detail here (see Klosko 1992, chaps. 3–4). An immediate difficulty is that there is great disagreement among theorists and citizens about what constitutes fair distribution. To address this problem, I believe we should appeal to fair procedures. In other words, I believe the question of fair distribution should be settled democratically.

Democratic procedures play an important role in fair-play obligations – as, I believe, it is likely they do in any reasonable theory of political obligation. Thus they should be discussed in some detail.

Political Obligations and Democratic Procedures

In recent years, prominent scholars have called attention to the role that democratic procedures play in grounding political obligations. Theorists who explore this subject focus on the need that laws be made in ways that protect equality. For example, in his important book on democracy, Thomas Christiano argues from what he calls concerns of "public equality." This requires not only that people be treated as equals, but also that institutions of society be structured "so that all can see that they are being treated as equals" (Christiano 2008, 2). Similarly, Daniel Viehoff (2014) argues that democracy is necessary in public deliberations to preserve equality. The need for democracy is especially clear when deliberations concern moral requirements binding on individuals: that is, in regard to political obligations. If people are morally required to accede to decisions, they should have a fair say in making them. This is particularly necessary in modern pluralistic societies in which people disagree strongly about the need for different laws and the form they should take. As we will see, I believe that democracy plays this role in regard to the fair-distribution requirement. However, in spite of democracy's essential contribution to political obligations, we should be clear on the fact that it itself is not able to ground them. In this section, I will explore the role that democracy does and does not play in political obligations. I will distinguish the view I maintain from one that claims that *the fact that a law is democratically made* is itself a reason to obey it.

In order to assess claims of democratic authority,

we must distinguish what we may call grounding and secondary reasons to obey particular laws. Grounding reasons create obligations directly. Thus if people consent to obey the law, the fact of consent is a grounding reason creating obligations for them to do so. Secondary reasons, in contrast, do not themselves create obligations but depend on grounding reasons, generally specifying their content. Thus if people consent, secondary reasons may be needed to fill in the content of what they have consented to. Having made this distinction, I believe we can see that, properly understood, the structure of democracy's contribution to political obligations is comprised of grounding reasons to obey the law provided by moral considerations other than democracy, while democracy supplements these, generally by determining their content.

An exhaustive analysis of the distinction between grounding and secondary reasons cannot be undertaken here. But a rough account should be adequate for our purposes. Consider an example. If Adam makes some promise to Beth, he has a clear grounding reason in regard to the content of the promise. Thus if he promises to take her to any Broadway show she chooses, he has a grounding requirement to do so. If she decides on *My Fair Lady*, he has a requirement to take her there. In this case, we can distinguish the secondary requirement to go to that particular show, as opposed to the grounding requirement to go to the show Beth chooses. Without Adam's prior promise to take her to the show of her choice, her opting for *My Fair Lady* would not bind him. I believe that, as a rule, the role of democratic procedures in regard to political obligations is along these lines. Accordingly, if Adam agrees to go to whatever show some civic organization decides on through democratic procedures, he is bound to accept their decision. But once again, the reason he is bound is his grounding agreement, with democratic procedures providing secondary reasons that fill in the content of his grounding requirement.

That democratic decisions do not bind in the absence of suitable grounding reasons can be demonstrated through examples. Does the fact that a group of my neighbors decides through some democratic process that all neighbors should go to a baseball game generate a requirement for me to go as well? Assume that I have not taken part in the deliberations. Obviously, in this case, the answer is no. But imagine that all people in the neighborhood had equal opportunities to participate in the deliberative process. All had opportunities for their views to be heard, and the decision was made fairly through majority rule. Still, this does not change things in regard to me. I am not bound even if I was granted a right to participate. In order for the decision to bind me, the issue in question must "apply" to me in some relevant way.[3] There are various ways in which a decision can apply to me, which turn on different grounding moral considerations. Most obviously, if I join or somehow bind myself to the decision procedure, then I have a moral requirement to abide by the result. For instance, suppose I meet with my neighbors and we all agree to take part in the activity that the majority decides on. Such a procedure is similar to that described by Locke, who argues that, when the community is first formed, majority decisions bind because people put themselves "under an obligation to everyone in that society to submit to the decisions of the majority, and to be bound by it" (1988 [1690], sec. 97). But according to Locke, one is bound only if one has consented to submit – though Locke of course employs an expansive notion of "consent."

Additional examples show that decisions can bind without pre-commitment, although other grounding reasons must be present. Imagine that my neighborhood faces some dire threat sufficient to trigger duties for all neighbors to take steps to avert

---

[3] The argument here draws on and so parallels that of Simmons against a natural duty of justice, in 1979, chap. 6.

it and that only coordinated action can be effective. Accordingly, the neighbors decide by majority rule to follow a specific plan of action. Under these circumstances, it is likely that all neighbors, including me, are bound to follow the decision, even if I and the others have not participated in the deliberations. Call this *Emergency*. However, once again, duties to go along with such a decision require more than its democratic nature. In this case, the reason I am bound is not the decision's democratic origin but my duty to help avert the disaster.

Under some circumstances, the content of grounding reasons can be filled in through means other than democracy. But it appears that these circumstances must preclude or otherwise tell against democratic decision making. Consider a plane crash. (Call this *Plane Crash I*.) A flight attendant is best positioned to get the passengers out safely if they coordinate their activities in accordance with her directions. Under these conditions, as David Estlund argues (2009, 124–5), it would be wrong for passengers not to obey her. In this case, passengers' duties to obey are triggered by their duties to help others in distress, and/or other similar moral principles.[4] Provided that listening to the flight attendant is the

---

[4] For the sense of "triggering," see Enoch 2011.

most likely way to fulfill these duties, the passengers have moral requirements to obey her, even though they are not able to deliberate and vote on how they should act. But what happens if circumstances do not rule out democratic decision making? Assume that it is necessary that everyone follow a single plan but listening to the flight attendant is not clearly the best or only way for everyone to be rescued. In this case, it seems that other people's opinions should be considered. If they deeply disagree, deciding among them through a fair vote should be the default option. Accordingly, let us revise the details (*Plane Crash II*). While the passengers are still in mortal danger, they decide by majority rule to follow such and such plan. Under these circumstances, it is safe to assume that Adam, who is a passenger, has a moral requirement to follow the plan, even if he has not participated in the deliberations or agreed beforehand to accept the results. But obviously, this is not because the plan was decided on democratically. As in *Emergency* and *Plane Crash I*, the decision binds him because of the need to take concerted action to deal with a crisis. Whether the plan of action is decided on democratically, as in *Plane Crash II*, or announced by the flight attendant, as in *Plane Crash I*, passengers are bound to comply with the decision because of these duties.

To conclude this excursion into democratic decision making, even though democratic procedures themselves do not create reasons to comply with decisions,[5] theorists have shown that they still make important contributions. This belief is strongly supported by moral intuitions according to which decisions that are not made democratically are suspect in regard to legitimacy.

On the construal defended in this section, democracy serves to satisfy moral conditions that legitimate laws must meet. Other necessary moral conditions include requirements that laws not be grossly immoral or significantly violate people's rights. Democracy satisfies requirements that laws be made fairly. All of these conditions must be satisfied if laws are to bind, but the latter do bind only if there are adequate grounding reasons.

The Content of Fair-Play Obligations

If we agree that democratic procedures are required to deal fairly with disagreement, we can see that they play an essential role in political obligations

---

[5] For an argument that democratic provenance generates reasons to *respect* decisions, including the law, though not to obey it, and what this entails, see Frye and Klosko 2017.

established by the principle of fair play. Because production of many goods involves complex systems in which large numbers of people are involved, democratic procedures must be appealed to if people are to be treated equally in regard to their preferences. This is necessary for deciding on what counts as fairness itself. In a diverse society, it is inevitable that people will disagree about this fundamental issue. This disagreement should be settled democratically. Through some fair democratic procedure, citizens should choose a principle of fair distribution from a possible list of acceptable principles. As long as the principle itself is recognized as being reasonably fair and is chosen fairly, if it is followed in practice, this should satisfy the fair-distribution requirement. In addition, to some extent, problems of fair distribution are lessened in regard to public goods because they generally fall out evenly throughout society. This is likely true of benefits such as national defense and clean air. Other public goods are more problematic. For instance, the security provided by law and order will likely vary considerably between areas – most likely, between richer and poorer areas. Thus steps should be taken to make things as even as possible (see Klosko 1992, 118–19). As discussed below in Chapter 5, if differences are too great and so condition (iii) is not or no longer satisfied, political obligations under fair play may be dissolved.

To a certain extent, the appeal to democratic procedures pushes the problem of fair distribution back one level, as there is also considerable disagreement about what constitutes fair democratic procedures. But once again, this should be settled democratically. Acceptable procedures should be chosen democratically from a list of suitable procedures. A certain degree of status quo bias is unavoidable in this position because, with existing democratic procedures used to make these determinations, some members of society may be advantaged if their preferences are favored by these particular procedures. But this is part of the price of coordinated activity necessary to provide essential public goods. Even with this additional cost included, in reasonably just states, I believe the distribution of benefits and burdens of social cooperation may be distributed with acceptable fairness and benefits will outweigh costs for all or almost all members of society most or almost all of the time.

An additional complexity is that presumptive public goods may be provided in many different ways, with their benefits and burdens varying accordingly. For example, in a large modern society, we may assume that citizens disagree about defense. Some people support a large, traditional military, while others prefer heavy use of targeted drones and increased reliance on special forces. Some people believe there are good reasons to invade other countries such as Iraq or North Korea, while others believe such a policy is catastrophically misguided. As a rule, coordinating activities in society requires imposition of uniform rules in each area. Consider the problem of setting speed limits or deciding the side of the road on which people should drive. Obvious reasons of safety and convenience require coordination on these issues and that the policies decided on must be reasonable. But once again, we may assume that people disagree on which policies would be optimal. The only way people can be treated fairly is if these issues are decided through fair democratic procedures (see esp. Christiano 2008).

A possible response to this argument concerns people who do not believe they benefit from these goods, or even if they do benefit, they would prefer to provide them themselves. In responding to this objection, we encounter difficult empirical or sociological issues. Is it really possible for people to provide law and order themselves, without intervention by the state? In regard to national defense, this possibility seems far-fetched. But what of law and order and the other presumptive goods discussed above? In this context, I cannot address these issues in detail. But once again, a basic assumption of my argument is that the state is necessary, that people could not successfully fend for themselves, especially in highly complex modern societies. However, alternatively, opponents of government could simply reject its benefits, because they dislike government provision or reject the goods under discussion for other reasons. I believe this latter question can be responded to relatively easily (see Klosko 2013). Is it true that many people *really* don't want the benefits of national defense or clean air? It's easy for people to say they don't want them, or even actually to believe that they don't want them. Such beliefs do not involve costs, as the benefits are public goods and so will be received more or less regardless of what people say or believe. But more than this, if such beliefs absolve one of obligations one would otherwise have, there are obvious benefits to holding them, with the result that people who hold these beliefs will be justified in free-riding. In response to such cases, we require some means to test the sincerity or defensibility of people's beliefs. At the very least, they should be able to pass what we may call an "alternative test." Subjects must be able to explain how they would cope without the benefits in question. While a pacifist would perhaps be able to pass this test in regard to defense – responding that, for religious reasons, she does not care how she would cope – I believe such cases will be rare, and so do not affect the principle of fair play's ability to satisfy the generality standard.

However, even if an argument succeeds in regard to presumptive goods, modern states do much more than this. Central tasks of governments include building roads, educating children, preserving the environment, providing museums and recreational facilities, and much more. Are all these tasks essential for acceptable lives? If not, does this mean that citizens are not required to obey laws that pertain to them? Alternatively, what if citizens genuinely do not want these benefits, or, perhaps more likely, do not want government to provide them? Since these benefits, unlike presumptive goods, are not necessary for acceptable lives, rejecting them is more plausible.

I view this as a serious problem. Extending the principle of fair play to encompass cooperative schemes that provide goods that are not presumptively beneficial involves considerable complexities, to which we turn in the following chapter.

4

Multiple-Principle Theory

The problem we have noted concerns the requirement that political obligations be "comprehensive," that a theory establish moral requirements to obey all laws passed by the state. Closely related is the idea of "content-independence," that laws bind because of their provenance rather than their content. If the only laws that citizens must obey concern the provision of essential public goods, then this feature of political obligations too is lost. In addition, content-independence is linked to the "self-image of the state," according to which the state is able to pass laws on any subject, thereby obligating citizens to obey. This too is not realized if the state is able to bind subjects only to the provision of essential public goods. Can the principle of fair play establish a successful theory if it is not able to move beyond these difficulties?

Multiple Principles

I believe a successful theory can be constructed, but in order to accomplish this we must to some extent redefine our standards of success. In particular, we must combine the principle of fair play with other moral principles in what we may call a "multiple-principle" theory (MP theory, for short).[1] Working out this theory requires moving away from widely held assumptions about theories of political obligation.

Although at first sight a multiple-principle approach might seem odd, there are strong considerations in its favor. In order to appreciate these, it is necessary to consider what a "theory" of political obligation actually is. In the literature, scholars commonly appeal to "theories" of political obligation based on particular principles. Some of these have been discussed in previous chapters. Thus Harry Beran (1987) has worked out a "consent theory of political obligation." and A. D. M. Walker (1988) has developed a theory based on gratitude. If we pause to think about what scholars mean by this locution, we will see that a "theory"

---

[1] See J. Wolff 2001 and Klosko 2004, for defense of a multi-principle or pluralistic approach.

of political obligation is a set of linked considerations intended to provide answers to questions concerning whether we have moral requirements to obey the law. Different positions are identified as "consent theory," "gratitude theory," "fair-play theory," because the reasons in question center upon the eponymous moral notions.

The goal of such theories is of course to provide reasons why we should obey the law. A successful theory establishes a strong presumption in favor of obedience, placing a burden of justification on people who claim that they need not obey. This much is fairly clear. However, we should also recognize that appeal to one of the moral notions indicated should not ordinarily rule out appeal to others. In most cases, there will be no incompatibility between, say, reasons to obey the law based on consent and on gratitude or a natural duty of justice, or other principles. If a theory based on a single principle is successful, we will generally not feel a need to move beyond that principle. For example, if a theory based on consent is thought to provide satisfactory reasons, we will not appeal to gratitude as well.

I believe, however, that discussion of these matters has developed in an overly rigid manner. In the literature, the different theories of obligation are often treated in reified form as independent "theories." Each is assessed as if it alone is to provide satisfactory answers to the full range of questions. When a given "theory" is found deficient in some respect, it can be labeled unsatisfactory and rejected. The critic can then move on to assess the next "theory" on his list. An indication of this form of argument was seen above in our treatment of consent theory, which falls short in terms of generality. This form of argument is a staple of the literature (Smith 1973; Simmons 1979; Raz 1989; Huemer 2012). Conclusions based on this procedure of "divide and conquer" are largely responsible for the currently widespread view that there is no satisfactory theory of political obligation.

That divide and conquer is flawed becomes apparent if we recognize that many different moral considerations can be relevant to questions of political obligation. The fact that no single moral principle is able to generate all required answers does not rule out the possibility that, if we supplement a given principle with other considerations, better answers can be developed. For instance, just because the principle of fair play is not able to establish political obligations that are comprehensive does not mean that it is unable to establish any at all. Accordingly, it may be possible to build upon the success that it does have by combining it with additional moral principles and so to construct a theory that is stronger than any based on a single moral principle. I believe that many political obligations are overdetermined and so there is an element of truth in many different theories of obligation. While the overlap of different principles complicates the task of laying out a satisfactory theory, the full range of laws could well be covered by a cross-hatch of different principles.

In working out a multiple-principle theory, I focus on what I view as the main practical problem of political obligation, explaining why citizens (most or all citizens) have moral requirements to obey the law (most or all laws). As we will see, other features of political obligations as commonly understood have to be set aside if this central task is to be accomplished.

Extending the Principle of Fair Play

To some extent, the problem of moving from obligations in regard to presumptively beneficial public goods to other state benefits can be overcome by what we may call "the indirect argument." If the state is to provide the indispensable goods noted above, society must possess a basic infrastructure – for example, transportation and communication facilities – to be able to do so. There cannot be adequate law enforcement or national defense unless there are adequate roads, bridges, airports, and so on. Fully filling out the indirect argument would involve many complexities that cannot be addressed here (but see Klosko 1992, chap. 4). I will confine attention to two points. First, the specific package of services in community C, required contributions to which can be grounded on the principle of fair play, depends on the specific indispensable goods the government of C provides. For ease of reference, we may label a good that government might provide that is not indispensable as "discretionary." According to the indirect argument, the citizens of C can be required to contribute to a given discretionary good if it can be shown to be part of a package of such goods that is required if C's government is to provide a given public good that is indispensable to their welfare. For instance, in the contemporary world, adequate national defense requires sophisticated industrial and scientific infrastructure. Obligations to support provisions for the relevant industries to function effectively can be justified, as can similar requirements in regard to facilities for various kinds of research and resources for scientific education. Law enforcement requires adequate roads and communication facilities and what is necessary to support them. And so obligations in regard to these can be justified as well, although, once again, the specific discretionary goods that can be justified cannot be identified on an abstract level but depend on the indispensable goods that are provided..

The problems in determining the precise contents of a given package of discretionary goods are compounded by the pluralism and diversity of modern liberal societies. As with presumptively beneficial public goods, citizens are likely to disagree about the discretionary goods that are necessary to enable their provision. In keeping with the discussion in the previous chapter, such disagreements should be settled by fair democratic procedures, with the added check that the results should be defensible with strong reasonable arguments. If we grant these claims, then the principle of fair play is able to establish obligations to support a range of indispensable goods and a package of discretionary goods that is indirectly necessary for the former's provision, as determined in this manner.

The resulting position possesses a significant strength, but also a significant disadvantage. Although this argument allows us to encompass a much wider range of laws than those in regard to essential benefits alone, it is far from establishing obligations in regard to all laws. Modern states perform innumerable services that cannot be justified as necessary for presumptive goods. Thus even with the indirect argument included, the principle of fair play falls short in regard to the requirement of comprehensiveness. Hence the need for multiple principles.

An important class of benefits that the principle appears to be unable to support concerns services that benefit *other* people. The principle of fair play as discussed to this point can be described as a "self-benefit principle" (Arneson 1982). Throughout our discussion, fair-play obligations have been justified on the basis of benefits obligees themselves receive, which accounts for central aspects of the position developed: for example, that benefits must be worth their costs to recipients and that the latter do wrong to receive them without bearing their fair share of the burdens necessary to produce them. But states perform a range of services that oftentimes do not benefit taxpayers – contributors – themselves. Notable examples include social welfare services that support the poor, handicapped, or otherwise disadvantaged.[2] Up to a point, such services can be

[2] The provision under discussion is necessary when these groups are unable to make the contributions required of other citizens. In addition, I do not contend that these

viewed as public goods. To the extent that they keep the poor minimally satisfied and so not disruptive of public order, they contribute to the overall environment of law and order that is beneficial to everyone. But welfare functions ordinarily go beyond this, and to the extent that they benefit only recipients, they require justification by other moral principles.

A second area concerns benefits that are obviously discretionary and not covered by the indirect argument. Governments typically regulate their economies to keep inflation and unemployment in check, a function that, although highly desirable, is arguably neither indispensable for satisfactory lives nor necessary for the provision of essential public goods. Perhaps less consequential, governments support recreational and cultural activities: public parks, wilderness areas, museums, operas, symphonies, and the like. Moreover, public parks, opera houses, symphonies, and so on, are excludable services. They can be withheld from specific people relatively easily through admission or other similar provisions. Thus it is not clear if the principle of fair play can justify that people who do not choose to make use of them be required to support them.

services must be provided, but only that, if the state does provide them, general obligations to contribute to them can be justified within an MP theory.

Although the principle of fair play has difficulty establishing obligations in these areas, other principles can fill the gap. I will discuss two principles: a duty of mutual aid, which requires people to help others who are in severe need or distress; and an extension of the principle of fair play itself – giving rise to what we might term a "two-stage" fair-play theory.

In the literature, the duty of mutual aid is most commonly discussed in connection with the so-called "natural duties of justice," presented by John Rawls in *A Theory of Justice* (1999, secs. 19 and 51). According to Rawls, natural duties are unlike obligations in that they bind all people without regard to their voluntary actions. If Abe makes a promise to Beth, the obligation binds only Abe and is owed only to Beth. Other people not involved in the transaction through which the obligation is generated neither owe nor are owed what has been promised. With a natural duty, in contrast, all individuals are bound by the requirement in question, which is also owed to all people. For example, all people have duties of mutual aid to assist anyone who is in need or distress. Several of Rawls's natural duties are familiar, intuitively clear moral principles. These include the duty not to harm or injure others (1999, 98), the duty to show others the respect due to them as moral beings (297), and mutual aid, "the duty of helping another when he is in need or jeopardy, provided that one can do so without excessive risk or loss to oneself" (98).

In Rawls's theory, the status of the natural duties rests on the fact that they would be adopted by the representative individuals in the original position. However, setting aside the details of Rawls's arguments, I view the natural duties as intuitively clear moral principles, which can be assumed to hold. I take it as obvious that we recognize these principles as general moral requirements, binding on all people. For example, we generally recognize a requirement to aid a person in distress: for example, a child who is drowning in a swimming pool.[3] Other things being equal, for Abe to walk by and not aid the child would subject him to severe moral condemnation. The requirement to help other people who are in need or distress also applies to society's unfortunate members: for example, orphans, the mentally ill, the handicapped, and others who cannot care for themselves

In *A Theory of Justice*, Rawls attempted to establish a full theory of political obligation based on

[3] An excellent defense of such a duty is provided by Feinberg 1984, 126–86; for laws of different countries in regard to such requirements, see Klosko 2005, 95–7.

what we may call the "natural political duties." He introduced two political duties: duties "to comply with and to do our share in just institutions"; and to assist in establishing just institutions when they do not exist (1999, 293–4; similarly, 99). Because they apply to everyone, if accepted, Rawls's argument could establish general political obligations, and many theorists view a natural-duty approach as a promising way to ground a successful theory of obligation.[4] However, even if we accept the existence of the natural political duties, there is a problem with this line of argument. The natural duties are generally conceived of as having limitations on their force. Thus according to Rawls, the duty of mutual aid is to help others when they are in need, "provided that one can do so without excessive risk or loss to oneself" (1999, 98). The duty to bring about a great good holds "only if we can do so relatively easily" (100). The second of the natural political duties, the duty to help establish just institutions, is similarly qualified (294, 99).[5]

---

[4] Waldron 1993; Wellman 2001 and 2005; Christiano 2008; Ripstein 2009; Stilz 2009; for criticisms, see Klosko 1994; Simmons 2005.

[5] It is not clear that Rawls recognizes the implications of holding that his second political duty is cost-qualified, while the first is not (see Klosko 1994). Wellman's principle of Samaritanism is similarly cost-qualified (2001, 744, 748,

Our general intuitions concerning the natural duties support the claim that they are of limited force. As we have noted, Abe would be severely condemned if he allowed a child to drown. The same would be true if rescuing the child would require him to get his clothing wet, even to ruin his expensive shoes. But ordinarily, we would not say that his duty to assist the child would require significant risk: for example, if he had to rush into a burning building that might collapse at any time. Actions of this kind pass beyond the required to the supererogatory and are the stuff of heroism.

If this contention is granted, then we can see the limitations of a theory of political obligation based solely on the natural duties. Requirements to comply with just institutions as long as this is not costly to oneself would not ground obligations to pay burdensome taxes or to obey other costly laws, let alone to undertake military service, to fight, possibly to die, for one's country. However, even if a natural-duty view cannot serve as a self-standing theory of political obligation, it can contribute significantly to a multiple-principle theory, as we have formulated it. The natural duties could fill a

752 n. 21; see Wellman 2005, 17–19, 65–71). Waldron (1993) does not discuss the question of costs.

gap in the principle of fair play by supporting social welfare and other similar programs, as long as the burdens they pose are not onerous. One reason requirements along these lines are permissible is that they generally entail only financial contributions. Requiring that Abe contribute money to a homeless shelter is obviously less burdensome than requiring that he spend time there: for example, making beds or counseling clients. As long as financial contributions are reasonably light, the principle of mutual aid should be able to generate requirements for many programs. In the abstract, it is difficult to draw the line between acceptably light and objectionably heavy burdens. Perhaps something along the lines of the 10% tithe that many religions impose (or suggest) is acceptable. Perhaps the level should be lower, only 2% or 3%, while the amount that can be required will depend to some extent on the level of need and the kind of services that can be provided. Once again, this matter, like the content of political obligations generally, should be settled by democratic procedures. Whatever the difficulties in identifying precise lines here, a theory of political obligation that combines the principle of fair play and some variant of the duty of mutual aid can be stronger than a theory built on either of these principles taken separately. But before we accept this position fully, we must address an important problem: the "particularity" of obligations under natural duty (Simmons 1979, 31–5).

As noted in Chapter 1, central to common notions of political obligation is a strong connection between the individual and the specific political body of which he is generally a citizen. In the literature, this aspect of political obligations is referred to as "particularity." However, this is difficult for a duty of mutual aid to account for. If Beth is required to help people in distress, why must these be her fellow citizens, as opposed to allowing her to fly off to Africa or East Asia, where people are likely in far greater distress? If, following Rawls, we recognize a natural political duty "to comply with and to do our share in just institutions when they exist and apply to us" (1999, 293), then it has to be explained why Beth must comply with the institutions of one country rather than another. Even though she lives in Great Britain, which we may assume possesses just institutions, Sweden, Canada, and Belgium may also be assumed to have just institutions. Why must she comply with and support the British government, rather than the governments of these countries? This problem seems to be addressed in Rawls's formulation as a duty to support just institutions when they "apply" to us (1999, 293). But this of course raises the question of how institutions "apply" to one (Simmons 1979, chap. 6).

In the literature, various means have been proposed to overcome the particularity problem (e.g., Goodin 1988; Waldron 1993; Wellman 2000). The most convincing, I believe, are rooted in reciprocity. One advantage of combining different moral principles is that this can provide means to identify the political community of which one is a member and so the institutions that apply to one. Because individuals could not lead acceptable lives without indispensable benefits provided by the community, it is misleading to think of them as isolated individuals in the equivalent of a Lockean state of nature. Beth is "naturally" a member of the community that supplies her with indispensable goods. The institutions that "apply" to her are those that provide these goods, and she has special responsibilities towards her fellow citizens, because their efforts are necessary for essential public goods she receives.

If we accept the argument in the last paragraph, then obligations under the principle of fair play are able to avoid the particularity problem. But what of natural duties of mutual aid to assist the poor and unfortunate? Why do these hold in regard to the poor of one's own country rather than others, in which people are likely to have greater needs? This problem too can be solved if we recognize that the specific natural duties under discussion should not be considered in the abstract but exist in a particular context. To begin with, return to the importance of democratic decision making. As we have seen, through the principle of fair play, people have moral requirements to contribute to the goods they receive. Not only the fair-distribution requirement but also commonsense concerns of fairness and equity require that people whose liberty is limited by specific provisions have a fair say in shaping them. As noted above, in a diverse society, people will inevitably disagree about the form in which presumptive public goods are provided. All who are bound should have an equal say over the nature of these provisions, which requires fair democratic decision making. Obviously there must be political equality, as expressed in familiar maxims such as "one man one vote," and "all votes should be counted equally." Citizens also require access to necessary means of effective participation, for example freedom of speech and association, and must be able to engage in political activities safely and without harassment. These points go almost without saying. In addition to requirements of political equality is a related need for some measure of economic equality, because rights to democratic participation must be not only formal but substantive. It is not enough for citizens simply to possess rights to participate in the relevant decision processes. These rights must be able to be exercised in an effective manner. If citizens lack basic education or have no time or resources to become informed, politically active citizens, whatever political rights they have cannot be effectively exercised. These considerations require that citizens have a certain level of material resources. Bare subsistence is not enough. Citizens require what we may call an adequate level of income – adequate to allow them leisure to become informed about political affairs – along with sufficient education to make it possible for them to do this and to participate actively.[6] Unless all citizens have such resources, they will be treated unfairly in the schemes of cooperation to which they are required to contribute. Accordingly, we should recognize special requirements of justice in regard to one's fellow citizens that do not hold in regard to inhabitants of other countries. How these are to be weighed against duties to come to the aid of the poor and suffering in other countries

[6] See Rawls's discussion of the equal worth of the political liberties and other requirements these entail (1999, 197–9; 2002, 148–50).

is a question that can be set aside here, as long as we recognize these particularized duties to assist the poor of one's own country.

An additional consideration is that, as noted above, only if the poor and unfortunate members of society regularly obey the law can there be an overall atmosphere of law and order that is essential to everyone's well-being. The efforts of all, including the unfortunate, are also necessary for the provision of national defense, successful working of public health, environmental measures, and the like. These considerations also support duties to assist the poor in one's own country rather than needy members of other societies. Thus I conclude that the duties of mutual aid under discussion can be directed at inhabitants of one's own country, and so adequately particularized.

If we accept these claims, then the resulting theory makes considerable strides in regard to the comprehensiveness criterion. While the principle of fair play primarily justifies requirements that pertain to programs that are beneficial to individuals themselves, the duty of mutual aid can require citizens to support social welfare and related programs that benefit unfortunate members of their society. Because the need to care for the poor and distressed is a moral requirement of all inhabitants of community C, all are required to do their fair share in whatever institutions are set up to fulfill these functions. Thus each citizens should contribute her or his fair share to this additional set of communal burdens.

Two-Stage Theory of Fair Play

The theory of political obligation developed thus far still falls short of the comprehensiveness requirement. As I have noted, in addition to providing indispensable public goods and seeing to the needs of the unfortunate, all modern states provide a large range of other services. Not only do they regulate their economies, but they also supply public education, museums, symphonies, national parks, and innumerable other benefits. An additional consideration concerns the existence of a standing mechanism to take measures for the common good. As Hume says, once government has been established, it is able to take on additional tasks. Although certain projects are clearly in the public interest, they are often too large for one or a few persons, while, without government, it is difficult to marshal the efforts necessary to achieve them. Government is able to get things done, and so to provide great benefits for the community: "Thus bridges are built, harbours open'd, ramparts rais'd, canals form'd, fleets equip'd," and other ends accomplished, which would not have been possible without government intervention (Hume 1969 [1739], 590 [III, ii, 8]). Each of these projects might not be either indispensable, indirectly necessary for the provision of indispensable goods, or required by a principle of mutual aid. But because each one contributes to society, an extended principle of fair play is able to justify them and others. More fundamentally, a policy that makes it possible to provide these services should on the whole benefit all members of the community. As Hume suggests, a mechanism that coordinates the energies and activities of citizens for the common good should be viewed as presumptively beneficial for almost all if not all members of society (see Den Hartogh 2002, chap. 5)

The need for democratic decision making can be extended beyond essential public goods and social welfare provisions. What exactly this mechanism – i.e., government – is to do should be decided democratically. As with the areas we have discussed, democratic processes are necessary to settle disagreements on matters that affect the public good throughout society. However, because many matters that fall within this category are not essential for acceptable lives, it follows that democratic procedures to adjudicate them are also not indispensable, and so cannot be defended on the basis of the fair-play argument in the previous chapter.

Our question, then, is whether MP theory can be extended to support these activities. What we require is a second-stage version of the principle of fair play, to which I will refer as FP2. According to this principle, citizens have moral requirements to support the democratic political mechanism in place in community C and to comply with its decisions, as it settles disagreements on indispensable and other necessary public goods[7] and programs for the unfortunate, and as it takes reasonable measures to promote the common good in other ways.

As discussed in the previous section, FP2's ability to create binding moral requirements follows from the fact that supply of indispensable public goods under the principle of fair play creates a community. Once again, the independent, Lockean individual in the state of nature is a fiction. Because Beth and other inhabitants of society could not lead acceptable lives

---

[7] For convenience, in various contexts below, I will not mention supply of necessary discretionary goods covered by the indirect argument along with goods that are themselves indispensable. Their inclusion can be assumed.

without public goods supplied by joint cooperation, they should be viewed as "naturally" members of the community that supplies them. The argument here resembles Aristotle's famous account of man as a "political animal" in Book I of the *Politics* (Bk. I, chap. 2; 1253a1–3; see Klosko 2012, 126–9). Because Beth and other inhabitants of contemporary states are able to lead acceptable lives only if they are members of political communities, in order to provide necessary public goods, she and other members of community C must develop effective decision-making institutions. With these institutions in place, members of C can employ them to advance their further interests. Not every project that C undertakes needs to be either indispensable or necessary under the natural duties of justice. But because each one contributes to the good of C and its members, FP2 justifies it. As with essential public goods, there is a strong presumption that all members of C benefit from the decision mechanism in question. Accordingly, it follows from the principle of fair play that if Beth and other inhabitants of C benefit from the joint efforts of their fellows in regard to these measures, then they have moral requirements to do their fair shares in providing them. For ease of reference, we will refer to the entire range of programs FP2 supports as "common provisions."

According to familiar political intuitions, there is little doubt that governments are justified in providing for the health and welfare of their populations, regulating their economies, and taking other measures that are clearly in the public interest. All reasonably decent modern states pursue these ends, and we would likely raise questions about a government that did not do so. In general, citizens' main responsibilities in supporting such programs are paying taxes. The programs in question are costly, and citizens have moral requirements to contribute their fair shares. Imagine that tax payments are clearly divided so that the amount each citizen pays for each program can be clearly identified. Under such circumstances, Abe will be required to contribute the requisite amount to each program that can be properly justified. He will be morally required to do his fair share to support programs that not only benefit him but also advance the good of the community of which he is a member.

Before proceeding, we should note that if it can be established along these lines, FP2 might appear to be *too* successful. Provision of indispensable public goods and necessary discretionary goods may be viewed as clearly in the public interest, as may programs to aid the unfortunate. If the community votes to supply them, then they will appear to fall under FP2. If this is true, then FP2 itself may satisfy the comprehensiveness requirement, thereby making MP theory unnecessary. However, FP2 by itself is not able to fulfill this role. FP2 requires prior delineation of the community of which one is a member. As I have noted, this is provided by joint production and consumption of indispensable public goods under the principle of fair play. Without this, it is not clear exactly what makes Beth a member of a specific community and why she must support efforts to advance its interests as opposed to those of other polities. However, as for programs to meet the needs of the poor and unfortunate, these may well be supported by FP2. Once again, I do not see any difficulty in recognizing that different moral principles may overlap in regard to supporting particular political obligations. But it seems advisable to distinguish FP2 and the natural-duty principle discussed in the previous section, for reasons we have seen. Like the principle of fair play itself, FP2 is a self-benefit principle and so should be distinguished from the natural duties, which primarily benefit other people. Although the MP theory developed in this work is closely related to a theory of obligation based on a single moral principle, characterizing it as a multiple-principle theory makes its inner logic more clear.

If we accept the argument to this point, we should recognize qualifications and conditions that FP2 should be required to satisfy. Once the relevant community is identified, its members can work jointly to promote its interests. Although FP2 might appear to justify sweeping measures that could dangerously impinge on citizens' liberties, it is circumscribed by the fact that measures must actually be in the community's interest. Unpacking this notion gives us three conditions that must be satisfied:[8]

(ia)   the government services or provisions in question must actually be in the public interest: that is, benefits must outweigh costs for society;

(iia)   benefits and burdens of these provisions must be distributed fairly;

(iiia) decisions in regard to these benefits must be made democratically, with all citizens having a fair say.[9]

---

[8] I believe justification of these requirements follows clearly from considerations discussed above.

[9] These conditions are closely related to those for the principle of fair play as discussed above, although of course without condition (ii). (iia) and (iiia) correspond to (iii), with that principle filled in in regard to the need for democratic decision making.

According to (ia), society will be able to generate obligations through FP2 only if policies actually are in the public interest. It must be possible to show that, for each common provision, benefits to the public outweigh costs, which means that this will also be true of the overall package of common provisions.

An obvious objection is that this standard will likely fail to be satisfied in the real world. Actual democratic politics are infected by special-interest legislation. Democratic safeguards do not prevent either special interests from enacting programs that favor the few at the expense of the many or the majority from compelling the minority to support its own favored programs. These are formidable difficulties, but we should recognize that FP2 does not justify all government enactments that purport to be in the public interest, but only those that actually do promote the common good. Beyond a certain point, a government that is used by the majority to exploit the minority becomes illegitimate. Possible responses to such circumstances are discussed in the following chapter. However, it would be wrong to expect governments to be perfect, or even to meet demanding standards of justice. The appropriate standard is tolerable or reasonable justice. Government's actions must be on the whole defensible, though exceptions should be accepted. While each common provision must be worth its costs to the community as a whole, this standard need not be met for each citizen. Citizens are bound to benefit more from some measures than from others. The overall package of common provisions will be acceptable according to this criterion, as long as the benefits and burdens from the package as a whole for each citizen are worth their costs.

In addition to being beneficial for society, (iia) common provisions must be distributed fairly. If city A receives extensive benefits, then city B should be treated similarly. Criteria for allocating resources should be reasonable and neutral between geographical and cultural areas. Once again, this requirement is in regard to the package of benefits as a whole rather than each specific benefit, although unnecessary unfairness in regard to the latter is of course to be avoided. But each common provision should be regarded as a component of the overall package. Unfair distribution of specific components is not sufficient to justify disobeying specific laws let alone dissolving people's political obligations, as long as the overall package of benefits is reasonably fair and for each citizen.

Because obligations under FP2 draw on prior

obligations under the principle of fair play, it is essential that common provisions not upset these balances. If these conditions are not met, at some point, people's political obligations will be dissolved. Once again, we will discuss citizens' recourse in the following chapter.

Even if the overall distribution of common provisions is reasonably fair, individual citizens might easily object about specific goods necessary to advance the public interest, and could well believe that none are necessary at all. In diverse societies disagreements are expected; there will be an enormous range of opinions about what society requires. As we have noted, such decisions must be made through democratic procedures, which provide all members equal say (requirement [iiia]). As in regard to other issues, with people disagreeing about steps that should be taken to advance the general interest, their differences should be discussed and voted on, according to recognized procedures. It is not unlikely that many people will object to each decision that is made. The compromises required in a diverse society may well be to some degree unsatisfying to everyone alike. However, regardless of departures from their preferences, all individuals have obligations to support the result, as long as it is determined fairly and can be defended as on the whole reasonably fair and beneficial to society. FP2 in effect leaves all members of society subject to common determination of what is in the public interest. Although all do not consent to government, as Locke says, they are to be "concluded by the majority." But the obverse of this is that all inhabitants are able to attempt to persuade the majority to realize their own views of what is beneficial.

These considerations should be able to dispel objections of almost all individuals. Imagine that, even with the safeguards we have noted in place, Beth believes that, because the goods in question are not indispensable to her welfare or required to aid other people in distress, she should not be required to support their provision. We may hypothesize that she benefits relatively little from specific provisions and so could well believe that they are not worth their costs *to her*. The response is that while each specific provision might not benefit her, it is overwhelmingly likely that she will benefit from the overall package of benefits, as long as the three conditions are satisfied. The possibility remains that, for whatever reasons, she still does not benefit from the overall package. And so, as with other obligations discussed throughout this work, Beth's obligations to support FP2 are only presumptive. If she is able to make a strong case that she really does not benefit from FP2's provisions, then she may be absolved of her obligations to support them – and, conceivably, of her political obligations altogether.

I should note how unlikely I believe such cases will be. Because Beth is a member of society, if she objects to a specific provision (call it P), its defenders can reply that her way of conceptualizing her situation is doubly incorrect – wrong in two different respects. In objecting to having to support P, Beth is likely to construe the situation as whether she as a distinct individual is morally required to contribute to a distinct government benefit. But for reasons we have seen, Beth is not a distinct individual; she is a member of society, while P is not a distinct benefit but part of an overall package of benefits that society provides through a process of deliberating about appropriate means to promote the general good.

Consider Nozick's example of the public-address system (1974, 93–5; see pp. 45–6 above). As we have seen, Nozick would argue that Beth does not have an obligation to support this system unless she agrees to do so. However, once again, the public address system does not stand by itself. It is part of a package of benefits that is viewed as in the general interest by the community itself, of which Beth is a member and in the deliberations of which she has rights to participate. Because of C's democratic institutions, Beth is like other C-ites in having the ability to attempt to influence her fellow citizens to utilize public resources to promote what she believes to be the common good. Only if she could argue that, in spite of all this, she does not benefit from the common provisions as a package could she be freed of her obligation to support them.

It could be objected that since the public-address system is a detachable part of C's overall package of benefits, C is not justified in extending the obligations Beth has in reference to other goods to the public-address system as well. As Simmons argues, if a provider of a given set of goods extends his provision to include additional goods, "this should be at his own risk. He should either provide them free or try to make them excludable; what he may *not* do is impose them on others at a price set by him" (1987, 274; his emphasis). But although individual components of the package can be detached and provided separately, what links them is that all are specific applications of society's general effort to advance the common good. Once again, even if Beth does not benefit from the process in some particular case, in all likelihood she benefits from other aspects of the package, while she is also protected by the safeguards we have noted. If obligations to support particular elements could be ruled out simply because given individuals did not benefit from them, the mechanism could accomplish almost nothing (beyond providing goods discussed in the previous sections), and all would be far worse off. And once again, if Beth is exceptional in not benefiting from the overall package of benefits, then she can make this case and be freed of obligations to support them. But again, I view such circumstances as so unusual that they will not affect the generality criterion.

A final consideration concerns ideological or philosophical objections to FP2. For a strong individualist such as Nozick, FP2 could still be objectionable, even if the overall package of benefits was worth its costs in some objective sense. Let us assume that Abe has the strong commitment to individual autonomy commonly found among libertarian anarchists. Even if the package of benefits might be considered to be worth its costs according to standard cost–benefit calculations, it is not worth its costs to him, because he strongly objects to having government intrude unnecessarily in his life. Although he might prefer not to receive presumptively beneficial public goods either, in regard to them, his objection is defanged, as he could not live an acceptable life without them. In regard to FP2, this argument holds no purchase. By definition, the provisions it supports are not necessary for an acceptable life, and it is quite possible that Abe would prefer a less easy life without them than having to receive them from government.

The response here, once again, is that Abe is arguing from the standpoint of an isolated individual, along the lines of Locke's inhabitants of the state of nature (and also as in Nozick's theory). But for Abe, this standpoint is inaccurate. By virtue of the fact that he receives indispensable benefits from inhabitants of C, he is a member of C and so has moral ties to the community of which he is a part. Moreover, the highly developed conception of autonomy from which he argues[10] is also at least in large part a product of society. As Richard Dagger says (1997, chap. 3), autonomy is a capacity, the exercise of which depends on the actions of other people as well as oneself and can be developed only in a community. One could not live an autonomous life without the indispensable public goods provided by society. One's personality, including the capacity to be autonomous in the first place, is largely formed

[10] For philosophical anarchism based on a strong – overly strong – conception of autonomy, see R. P. Wolff 1970.

by society. One's culture provides the "spectacles" through which one views the world, which are necessary for the developed moral outlooks through which alone autonomous actions are possible (see Dworkin 1986, 228; Kymlicka 1996, 83). To use Dagger's words: "[N]o one becomes or remains autonomous without the assistance and cooperation of other people" (1997, 66).

For these reasons, claims based on Beth's strong conception of autonomy or similar values carry less weight than might at first appear. But still, because the moral requirements under discussion are only presumptive, if Beth is able to make a convincing case that she in fact does not benefit from common provisions or should be freed of her obligations in their regard for other reasons, then she will be.

Assessment

If we grant the arguments in the previous sections, then the result is a theory that satisfies the requirements presented in Chapter 1. MP theory is general, grounding obligations for most or all citizens, particular, and comprehensive, covering all justifiable services performed by the state. With its three moral principles intersecting and interacting, MP theory takes on a certain complexity. It becomes difficult to determine exactly where the contributions of one principle leave off and those of another begin. The fact that MP theory depicts many political obligations as grounded by more than one principle is perhaps disconcerting at first. But this is consistent with the initial intuitive plausibility of many different theories of political obligation and corresponds to the highly complex nature of contemporary societies.

Throughout this and previous chapters, we have discussed indispensable and discretionary goods as if they exist in isolation from one another and from social welfare services supported by natural duties and other services justified as promoting the common good. But in practice, these different functions overlap, with the workings of one affecting others, which in turn impact on others, and so on. The high degree of interpenetration is seen clearly in government's function of advancing the common good – much of which will overlap with functions justified by the other principles. This complex interweaving of moral principles corresponds to the complex, interconnected character of modern life. To have a safe and secure environment, an economy that functions healthily, efficient transportation and communication and other "essential services," in addition to amenities that make for more pleasant and interesting lives, requires a high degree of efficient coordination. The interdependence of different systems is readily seen when an element is not working smoothly – be it a power failure, a transportation workers' strike, a natural disaster, or a threat to public safety. There is room for disagreement as to whether the resulting disruptions are compatible with what we would view as "acceptable" lives. The complexities cannot be addressed here. But however we respond, it is clear that overlap and interactions between requirements to support the entire range of state functions match up with the overlapping nature of the functions themselves that are necessary for acceptable lives in modern societies.

At the beginning of this work, I noted that the theory that would be developed would depart from generally accepted assumptions about political obligations. This is obviously true as the multiple-principle nature of MP theory breaks from established tradition, which turns on examining individual principles apart from one another. As it seems to me, the turn to multiple principles is so strongly justified by common sense that it requires no additional defense. As noted above, many political obligations are overdetermined, justified by multiple considerations. This again seems so obvious as to require no defense.

An additional way in which MP theory departs from common assumptions is in rejecting the content independence of laws. In MP theory, reasons to obey laws follow from the moral principle we have laid out rather than the fact that they are laws. Because of these principles, I believe MP theory is able to fulfill the most important practical function of theories of political obligation and justify obedience to virtually all if not all legitimate laws. But this is not to say, as standard views have it, that a political obligation is a requirement not only to obey law L but to do so *because it is the law* (for many references, see Klosko 2011a). Many obligations established in MP theory are content-independent in a sense, but it is important to recognize that this is not in the precise sense envisioned in traditional theories of obligation. In order to see this, it is necessary to distinguish between: (a) moral reasons to behave as the law says to behave that are independent of content; and (b) moral reason to behave in this way for the content-independent reason that it is the law.

Consider a law bearing on national defense. As noted, national defense can take many forms. Assume that the inhabitants of C vote to invest heavily in special forces and drone warfare rather than in more aircraft carriers. For reasons we have seen, according to the principle of fair play, Abe will have moral requirements to obey law L that supports this provision. But if C had voted for aircraft carriers instead, his requirement would be to obey L2, which supports them. Obviously, then, his requirement to support L or L2 depends on the way in which they were established rather than their specific content. However, I do not believe Abe's obligation to support either law is content-independent in sense (b), *because it is the law*. Rather, his obligation is rooted in the principle of fair play: that he receives indispensable benefits from the cooperative efforts of his fellows and so has a duty to do his fair share in producing them. That it is this principle rather than the fact that L or L2 is the law that establishes his obligation is shown by the fact that other moral principles ground his obligations to obey other laws: those bearing on social welfare functions and common provisions, as discussed above. In the areas covered by each of these principles, content-independence in sense (a) holds. If different welfare programs or common provisions were decided upon, Abe would be required to obey the laws bearing on them instead. Thus in MP theory, requirements to obey the law have different bases. They are not consistent with the single ground *because they are the law*. And only if some component of MP theory justifies adherence to a particular law does Abe have requirements to obey it.

Although the state does not have the ability to bind us simply by making law, there are good reasons why it makes sense for it to claim to be able to do so, as in keeping with the traditional view of the self-image of the state. Even if people are not in fact bound by all laws simply because they are laws, it is oftentimes in their interest to believe that they are and to act accordingly. An important factor is cognitive errors to which people are liable, as discovered by recent psychological research (these are well discussed by Gur 2013). For example, "self-enhancement bias" leads people to overestimate their own capabilities and to underestimate their own incompetence, poor judgment, and other limitations. "Hyperbolic discounting" is people's tendency to overvalue immediate benefits or gratifications, as opposed to more remote benefits. These tendencies have been thoroughly documented empirically. Accordingly, even if people are well meaning and wish to pursue the public good, their judgment is often flawed. If they acted on their own conceptions of the public interest, they would likely err, with consequences that they and society as a whole would prefer to avoid. Thus the belief that we should obey the law because it is the law may often be a useful fiction, which would have desirable effects for society and its members, even if it cannot be supported by convincing arguments (Gur 2013). However, even if it is useful for people to believe that they have such obligations, this does not mean that they actually have them. Rather, people's political obligations are those that can be justified by moral principles, rather than those it would be helpful for them to believe they have. But once again, we have seen that, through a combination of moral principles, obligations for all citizens to obey all defensible laws can be established, even if these do not require that law be obeyed because it is the law.

5

Limits of Political Obligation

Having presented a theory of obligation that is able to justify moral requirements to obey all legitimate laws, we turn now to limitations of these obligations. Historically, the liberal tradition arose in attempts to limit what was perceived as unjust royal authority, and limitations were built into political theories from the outset. In this chapter, we will discuss such limitations and recourse when obligations are outweighed by countervailing moral considerations. This is a large topic, which could easily be the subject of its own volume. Discussion here must be general and avoid many complexities.

In regard to terminology, the limited nature of political obligations is noted in characterizing them as *prima facie* obligations, rather than conclusive obligations. What we mean by this designation is discussed above, in Chapter 1. As noted, the main idea is that obligations hold subject to the qualification "other things equal." By describing an obligation as *prima facie*, we are not saying that it is somehow not a genuine obligation.Although *prima facie* obligations are capable of being overridden by countervailing moral considerations, they may be presumed to hold in the absence of such considerations.

The political obligations discussed throughout this work may generally be assumed to be *prima facie* obligations. Although we may ordinarily assume that people subject to them have moral requirements to comply, these can be overridden by conflicting moral considerations or dissolved by unacceptable injustice. For instance, assume that Abe is serving in the army in accordance with a legitimate requirement that all citizens do so. But also assume that he is ordered to do something highly unjust, for example to execute unarmed civilians. I assume that, under most circumstances, his obligation would no longer hold, that he would do wrong if he complied – and would possibly also be liable to criminal prosecution. It could be a matter of dispute whether Abe's obligation in this case is overridden by injustice or dissolved. This is a question we need not examine. In either case, what interests us is the limited nature of the obligation.

The limited character of political obligations is a distinctive aspect of the liberal tradition. Throughout most of history, questions of political obligation were seldom raised (see Klosko 2011b). Among rulers and subjects alike, it was generally assumed that subjects had moral requirements to obey the laws or rulers' commands, and non-obedience was generally not discussed. This is true of ancient Greek political theory. Perhaps the only sustained examination of the subject in ancient Greek literature is found in Plato's *Crito*, in which Socrates considers the justice or injustice of escaping from prison to avoid execution – but decides he must obey the law. Although the early Christians generally argued for obedience, they devoted more attention to the subject and upheld an important limitation. In accordance with Jesus' commands to render unto Caesar what is Caesar's and to God what is God's (Matthew 22.21), and the injunction to obey God rather than man (Acts 5.29), they believed it was necessary *not* to obey commands that went directly against religious obligations. This condition was bound up with an important distinction between non-obedience or passive resistance and active or forcible resistance. Although injunctions that went against God's word were not to be obeyed, the subject was forbidden to resist forcibly and so had to accept the consequences of non-obedience, which often meant martyrdom. For instance, the *Martyrdom of Polycarp*, the earliest extant account of a Christian martyrdom, describes how the Roman Governor gave Polycarp a choice between recanting his beliefs or being burned alive. Polycarp chose the latter.

> The fire you threaten me with cannot go on burning for very long; after a while it goes out. But what you are unaware of are the flames of future judgment and everlasting torment which are in store for the ungodly. (*Martyrdom of Polycarp*, 11; in Staniforth 1968, 159)

In modern terms, the idea expressed here is frequently referred to as "conscientious refusal."[1] If some command or law is wrong – or, in many cases, goes against the subject's conscience – then he or she is justified in refusing to obey it. More important than obedience to the law is adherence to valid moral or religious principles, and to the latter, obeying the law should give way.

In itself, conscientious refusal does not entail additional steps that the subject takes. As noted, non-obedience could be met with severe penalties,

---

[1] A well-known account is presented by Rawls (1999, 323–4).

up to and including punishment by death. But conscientious refusal does not require specific response to penalties. Unlike civil disobedience, as we will see momentarily, conscientious refusal need not be a public act, and penalties need not be accepted. If someone can avoid obeying the law and not suffer for it, this does not change the nature of his or her refusal. For example, the actions of many Vietnam War draft avoiders could be described as conscientious refusal, even though they avoided punishment for not serving.

Civil disobedience differs from conscientious refusal in entailing specific additional behaviors. As generally understood, civil disobedience is not only a refusal to obey the law but also an attempt to change the law through public disobedience.[2] Rawls describes it as "a public, nonviolent, conscientious yet political act contrary to law usually done with the aim of bringing about a change in the law or policies of the government" (1999, 320). This measure is employed when its practitioner accepts the overall legitimacy of the regime and so does not engage in revolutionary activity intended to topple it, but objects to particular laws. Civil disobedience

---

[2] In spite of the title of Thoreau's famous work, "Civil Disobedience" (1993 [1849]), its subject is actually conscientious refusal.

must be public, because disobeying particular laws is intended to call attention to their injustice and so lead to desire to change them. Attempts of this nature require a degree of faith in the regime as a whole. Only if it is basically sound will it respond appropriately by attempting to remedy injustice, rather than simply crushing the protestors. Civil disobedience must also be peaceful, with the practitioner accepting punishment. This acknowledges overall faith in the regime, and attests to the purpose of disobeying the law. Notable examples in recent American history include reactions to racist Jim Crow laws: for example, that African Americans could not use various public facilities or had to ride at the back of buses. But rather than simply refusing to obey these laws, subjects called attention to their disobedience. In order to express their commitment to the regime as a whole, they allowed themselves to be punished, and also called attention to the punishment. In behaving in this way, the subjects attempted to raise awareness of the injustice of the laws in question, hoping to inspire public opposition to them and so to help change them. Civil disobedience, in other words, is an act of political communication. If the regime as a whole is acceptably just, it should have resources to allow it to change unjust laws, to bring them into accord with the overall justice of the regime.

This pattern was seen in the struggle for equal rights for African Americans, as many people were not only penalized for their actions but also publicized the penalties. For example, on so-called "Bloody Sunday," in 1965, civil rights proponents marched in support of voting rights from Selma, Alabama, to Montgomery, Alabama, in awareness that their actions would receive a violent police response. The widely televised sight of police beating peaceful protestors spurred public consciousness of racial injustice and contributed to passage of an important voting rights bill.

The non-violent nature of civil disobedience is famously associated with the work of Mahatma Gandhi, in India, whose example was emulated in the United States by Martin Luther King. Because this form of protest requires that the overall regime be acceptably just and the population at least potentially committed to remedying injustices, it is likely that this tactic will be successful only in liberal democracies. In 1989, when large numbers of Chinese demonstrated peacefully in Tiananmen Square, hundreds were massacred by the military. The degree of optimism about the regime that civil disobedience requires is not necessarily present with conscientious refusal. The latter is simple refusal to obey unjust laws, in many cases without hope of changing them.

If the regime is not acceptably just, a more extreme alternative is violent resistance or revolution, attempting to overthrow it. This notion has a distinguished place in the liberal tradition, as fomenting resistance to what he perceived as an unjust regime was central to Locke's purposes in his *Second Treatise* (see Ashcraft 1980). Similar concerns are central to the Declaration of Independence, which was based heavily on Locke, and of course written to justify a revolution. In general, a regime may be judged illegitimate on the basis of its conduct, generally, wholesale injustice or massive violation of people's rights. But it could also be unjust for procedural reasons, especially departure from democratic norms. In general, in order to command the allegiance of the population, a regime must be satisfactory in both dimensions. If a regime does not satisfy these standards and so is fundamentally unjust, revolution could be the only viable recourse. Civil disobedience will likely not work and may be met with overwhelming force, as was seen in Tiananmen Square.

Resort to revolution involves difficult questions concerning the precise point at which government should be judged sufficiently unjust to warrant this course of action and how exactly this determination should be made. To complicate matters further, in a diverse society, people are likely to disagree about the necessary degree of injustice, while, as recent events have shown, they are also likely to disagree about the facts of the case that might or might not make revolution necessary. These questions are extremely difficult and no clear formula exists to address them on an abstract level. It seems clear that monstrous regimes such as Nazi Germany or present-day North Korea are sufficiently unjust to warrant resistance by their subjects and revolution, if this is possible. But regimes that are less egregious raise issues that are more complex. For instance, consider the American South during the "Jim Crow" period. For decades, African Americans suffered from severe discrimination, but was the blatant injustice of so-called "Jim Crow" laws severe enough to justify toppling the government of the United States? To some extent, this question has received an answer from history, through the success of the less severe tactics used by civil rights activists. They apparently believed the regime was sufficiently just to allow racial injustice to be remedied through civil disobedience. But from the perspective of, say, Alabama or Mississippi in the 1920s, when treatment of African Americans was not only unjust but also supported by frequent lynchings and prospects for peaceful change were far from certain, was revolution justified? Once more, on such questions, people are likely to disagree.

To some extent these difficulties may be addressed by the separation of powers in a properly constituted government. According to standard doctrines of separation of powers and checks and balances, if an executive authority – e.g. a King or a President – rules unjustly, he may be removed from office by another branch of government, either the legislative branch or the courts. Under the US Constitution, determinations concerning the performance of government officials are in the hands of the legislative branch, with impeachment the main remedy. Two American Presidents were impeached (though not removed from office), while a third, Richard Nixon, was forced to resign from threat of impeachment. Under this process, Congress judges the President. A majority of the House of Representatives has the power to impeach the President, at which point he is tried by the Senate. If two-thirds of the Senate votes to remove him from office, the President is removed. Well-known examples in other countries concerned trials of King Louis XVI in France and Charles I in England – although one could question the legitimacy of these proceedings. In proceedings in which the legislature judges the executive, the former makes the determinations about the latter's guilt – in whatever ways deemed suitable. However, if these processes are conducted according to law or the constitutions of the relevant countries, they probably do not involve questions of political obligation, over and above normal requirements that everyone obey the law. Questions that go to the heart of political obligations arise when ordinary political processes are not able to deal with the circumstances, and so revolution becomes an alternative.

However, when we turn to revolution, without a legislative or other formal body to pass judgment on the executive, questions concerning the legitimacy of overthrowing the regime cause more difficulties. In a diverse society, people are likely to disagree on such issues, which makes these determinations all the more difficult. Locke's own position on these issues is radical in the extreme. He argues that, in the final analysis, each individual must judge for himself:

> [W]here the Body of the People, or any single Man, is deprived of their Right, or is under the Exercise of a power without right, and have no Appeal on Earth, there they have a liberty to appeal to Heaven, whenever they judge the Cause of sufficient moment. (1988 [1690], sec. 168)

[E]very Man is Judge for himself, as in all other Cases, so in this, whether another hath put himself into a State of War with him. (1988 [1690], sec. 241)

The logic here is clear. In the final analysis, each person must judge for herself. Even if there is in place a body to judge the government, it is always possible that you will disagree with its determinations. Thus if you are convinced that the existing US administration is fundamentally unjust and Congress is not taking appropriate action, then to whom can you turn? Locke is clear that you must have some recourse. No one is required to submit to unjust or arbitrary power, and so if there is no other remedy, you may take arms against the government, if you "judge the Cause of sufficient moment." But of course, unless large and powerful bodies of people feel similarly, you are unlikely to succeed. Locke himself thinks it unlikely that isolated individuals would actually take up arms against government: "[T]hough they have a right to defend themselves and to recover by force what through unlawful force has been taken from them, they will be disinclined to exercise their right by engaging in a contest in which they are sure to perish" (1988 [1690], sec. 208) As he says in the same section: it is "impossible for one or a few oppressed Men to disturb the Government," unless a large body of others believe themselves similarly aggrieved and are willing to act accordingly (sec. 208) But this concerns the practical side of revolution, as opposed to the moral question of when people are justified in rebelling.

Although questions concerning exactly when the injustice of a regime becomes sufficiently severe to remove political obligations are difficult to address in the abstract, if we base political obligations mainly on the principle of fair play, then questions concerning distribution of benefits and burdens of political membership become especially relevant. But once again, issues involved are bound to be controversial, including questions about the extent or nature of the inequalities for which government should be judged responsible. Especially, should government be held responsible for severe income inequality, or should this be attributed to factors in the economy that should be viewed as apart from government, or perhaps to differences in people's talents and abilities? Issues of discrimination raise fewer theoretical difficulties. Wherever one comes down on questions concerning the legitimacy or illegitimacy of the regime as a whole, a good case can be made that the people who suffer from discrimination should not be viewed as bound by specific laws that oppress them.

Consider conditions borne by residents in many American inner cities (see Shelby 2007). In spite of the country's commitment to formal equality and rhetoric of equal opportunity, these residents experience massive economic inequality, discrimination, and a harshly punitive criminal justice system. Their life prospects are markedly poorer than those of most other citizens, and while it is possible for some people to make it out of the "dark ghetto," this frequently takes extraordinary ability and resolve or good fortune. According to the principle of fair play, political obligations are rooted in basic notions of reciprocity, equal distribution of benefits and burdens of collective life. But what if the benefits and burdens are distributed so unequally throughout society that there is in effect no reciprocity? Under these circumstances, it is at least arguable that victims of discrimination do not have ordinary political obligations. Deviance may be a reasonable strategy. While it is difficult to justify violence against other people, it is at least arguable that victims of severe injustice do not have moral requirements to respect existing property laws, or laws against so-called "victimless crimes," for example prostitution and gambling. As Tommie

Shelby hypothesizes, "when the ghetto poor in the United States refuse ... to respect the authority of the law qua law, they do not thereby violate the principle of reciprocity or shirk valid civic obligations" (2007, 151).

Once again, questions along these lines are difficult for both empirical and moral reasons, but are an essential part of a full theory of political obligation.

References

Arneson, Richard J. 1982. "The Principle of Fairness and Free-Rider Problems." *Ethics*, 92: 616–33.

Ashcraft, Richard. 1980. "Revolutionary Politics and Locke's *Two Treatises of Government*: Radicalism and Lockean Political Theory." *Political Theory*, 8: 429–86.

Beran, Harry. 1987. *The Consent Theory of Political Obligation*. London: Croom Helm.

Broad, C. D. 1915–16. "On the Function of False Hypotheses in Ethics." *International Journal of Ethics*, 26: 377–97.

Christiano, Thomas. 2008. *The Constitution of Equality*. Oxford: Oxford University Press.

Dagger, Richard. 1997. *Civic Virtues*. Oxford: Oxford University Press.

Den Hartogh, Govert. 2002. *Mutual Expectations: A Conventionalist Theory of Law*. The Hague: Kluwer.

References

Dworkin, Ronald. 1977. *Taking Rights Seriously*. Cambridge, Mass.: Harvard University Press.

Dworkin, Ronald. 1986. *Law's Empire*. Cambridge, Mass.: Harvard University Press.

Enoch, David. 2011. "Giving Practical Reasons." *Philosophers' Imprint*, 11: 1–22.

Estlund, David. 2009. *Democratic Authority: A Philosophical Framework*. Princeton, NJ: Princeton University Press.

The Federalist: A Commentary on the Constitution of the United States. From the Original Text of Alexander Hamilton, John Jay, James Madison. n.d. New York: Modern Library.

Feinberg, Joel. 1984. *Harm to Others: The Moral Limits of the Criminal Law*, vol. 1. Oxford: Oxford University Press.

Frye, Harrison, and George Klosko. 2017. "Democratic Authority and Respect for the Law." *Law and Philosophy*, 36: 1–23.

Goodin, Robert. 1988. "What is So Special about Our Fellow Countrymen?" *Ethics*, 98: 663–86.

Green, Leslie. 1988. *The Authority of the State*. Oxford: Oxford University Press.

Green, Leslie. 1996. "Who Believes in Political Obligation?" In *For and Against the State: New Philosophical Readings*. John T. Sanders and Jan Narveson, eds. Lanham, Md.: Rowman & Littlefield.

Gur, Noam. 2013. "Actions, Attitudes, and the

Obligation to Obey the Law." *Journal of Political Philosophy*, 21: 326–46.

Harrod, R. F. 1936. "Utilitarianism Revised." *Mind,* 45: 137–56.

Hart, H. L. A. 1955. "Are There Any Natural Rights?" *Philosophical Review*, 64: 175–91.

Hart, H. L. A. 1958. "Legal and Moral Obligation." In *Essays in Moral Philosophy*. A. I. Melden, ed. Seattle: University of Washington Press.

Hart, H. L. A. 1961. *The Concept of Law*. Oxford: Oxford University Press.

Hart, H. L. A. 1982. "Commands and Authoritative Legal Reasons." In *Essays on Bentham*. Oxford: Clarendon Press.

Hobbes, Thomas. 1991 [1651]. *Leviathan*. Richard Tuck, ed. Cambridge: Cambridge University Press.

Huemer, Michael. 2012. *The Problem of Political Authority: An Examination of the Right to Coerce and the Duty to Obey*. Basingstoke: Palgrave Macmillan.

Hume, David. 1969 [1739]. *A Treatise of Human Nature*. Ernest C. Mossner, ed. Harmondsworth: Penguin.

Hume, David. 1985 [1748] "Of the Original Contract." In *Essays: Moral, Political and Literary*. Revised ed. Eugene F. Miller, ed. Indianapolis: Liberty Classics.

IRS Oversight Board. n.d.. "IRS Long Term Measures and Target Values." https://www.treasury.gov/IRSOB/measures/Documents/IRSOBMeasuresBooklet031215.pdf.

References

Kant, Immanuel. 1970 [1793]. "On the Current Saying: 'This May Be True in Theory, but It Does Not Apply in Practice.'" In *Kant's Political Writings*. H. Reiss, ed. H. Nisbet, trans. Cambridge: Cambridge University Press.

Klosko, George. 1991. "Reformist Consent and Political Obligation." *Political Studies*, 39: 676–90.

Klosko, George. 1992. *The Principle of Fairness and Political Obligation*. Savage, Md.: Rowman & Littlefield Publishers.

Klosko, George. 1994. "Political Obligation and the Natural Duties of Justice." *Philosophy and Public Affairs*, 23: 251–70.

Klosko, George. 2004. "Multiple Principles of Political Obligation." *Political Theory*, 32: 801–24.

Klosko, George. 2005. *Political Obligations*. Oxford: Oxford University Press.

Klosko, George. 2011a. "Are Political Obligations Content Independent?" *Political Theory*, 39: 498–523.

Klosko, George. 2011b. "Political Obligation." In *Oxford Handbook of the History of Political Philosophy*. George Klosko, ed. Oxford: Oxford University Press.

Klosko, George. 2012. *History of Political Theory: An Introduction*. 2nd ed. 2 vols. Volume I: *Ancient and Medieval*. Oxford: Oxford University Press.

Klosko, George. 2013. *History of Political Theory: An Introduction*. 2nd ed. 2 vols. Volume II: *Modern*. Oxford: Oxford University Press.

References

Klosko, George. 2018. "Consent Theory of Political Obligation." In *Routledge Handbook of the Ethics of Consent*. Andreas Müller and Peter Schaber, eds. Abingdon: Routledge.

Kymlicka, Will. 1996. *Multicultural Citizenship: A Liberal Theory of Minority Rights*. Oxford: Oxford University Press.

Locke, John. 1988 [1690]. *Second Treatise of Civil Government*. In *Two Treatises of Government*. Peter Laslett, ed. Student ed. Cambridge: Cambridge University Press.

Lyons, David. 1965. *Forms and Limits of Utilitarianism*. Oxford: Oxford University Press.

Nozick, Robert. 1974. *Anarchy, State, and Utopia*. New York: Basic Books.

Plamenatz, John. 1968. *Consent, Freedom, and Political Obligation*. 2nd ed. Oxford: Oxford University Press.

Rawls, John. 1999. *A Theory of Justice*. 2nd ed. Cambridge, Mass.: Harvard University Press.

Rawls, John. 2002. *Justice as Fairness: A Restatement*. Cambridge, Mass.: Harvard University Press.

Raz, Joseph. 1989. "The Obligation to Obey the Law." In *The Authority of Law*. Oxford: Oxford University Press.

Ripstein, Arthur. 2009. *Force and Freedom*. Cambridge, Mass.: Harvard University Press.

Shelby, Tommie. 2007. "Justice, Deviance, and the Dark Ghetto." *Philosophy and Public Affairs*, 35: 126–60.

References

Simmons, A. John. 1979. *Moral Principles and Political Obligations*. Princeton, NJ: Princeton University Press.

Simmons, A. John. 1987. "The Anarchist Position: A Reply to Klosko and Senor." *Philosophy and Public Affairs*, 16: 269–79.

Simmons, A. John. 2005. "The Duty to Obey and Our Natural Moral Duties." In *Is There a Duty to Obey the Law?* Christopher Heath Wellman and A. John Simmons. Cambridge: Cambridge University Press.

Singer, Peter. 1973. *Democracy and Disobedience*. Oxford: Oxford University Press.

Smith, M. B. E. 1973. "Is There a Prima Facie Obligation to Obey the Law?" *Yale Law Journal*, 82: 950–76.

Staniforth, Andrew L. M., ed. and trans. 1968. *Early Christian Writings*. Harmondsworth: Penguin.

Stilz, Anna. 2009. *Liberal Loyalty: Freedom, Obligation, and the State*. Princeton, NJ: Princeton University Press, 2009.

Thoreau, Henry D. 1993 [1849]. "Civil Disobedience." In *Civil Disobedience and Other Essays*. Phillip Smith, ed. Mineola, NY: Dover Publications.

Tyler, Tom. 1990. *Why People Obey the Law*. New Haven, CT: Yale University Press.

United States Election Project. n.d. "2016 November General Election Turnout Rates." http://www.elect project.org/2016g.

Viehoff, Daniel. 2014. "Democratic Equality and

Political Authority." *Philosophy and Public Affairs*, 42: 338–75.

Waldron, Jeremy. 1987. "Theoretical Foundations of Liberalism." *Philosophical Quarterly*, 37: 127–50.

Waldron, Jeremy. 1993. "Special Ties and Natural Duties." *Philosophy and Public Affairs*, 22: 3–30.

Walker, A. D. M. 1988. "Political Obligation and the Argument from Gratitude." *Philosophy and Public Affairs*, 17: 191–211.

Wellman, Christopher Heath. 2000. "Relational Facts in Liberal Political Theory: Is There Magic in the Pronoun 'My'?" *Ethics*, 110: 537–62.

Wellman, Christopher Heath. 2001 "Toward a Liberal Theory of Political Obligation." *Ethics,* 111: 735–59.

Wellman, Christopher Heath. 2005. "The Duty to Obey and Our Natural Moral Duties." In *Is There a Duty to Obey the Law*? Christopher Heath Wellman and A. John Simmons. Cambridge: Cambridge University Press.

Wolff, Jonathan. 2001. "Political Obligation: A Pluralistic Approach." In *Pluralism: The Philosophy and Politics of Diversity*. Maria Baghramian and Attracta Ingram, eds. London: Routledge.

Wolff, Robert P. 1970. *In Defense of Anarchism*. New York: Harper & Row.

Index

Index

Index

Index